my Ibiza experience

by

siriya gaia

dedication

I would like to dedicate this book to all the beautiful people who told me their fascinating stories that I am sharing here. Without them my story would only be half told.

acknowledgements

Many thanks to my ghost writer, Mary-Lynne Stadler, for all her work in helping me to put this book together so coherently and articulately. I could not have done it without her. Many thanks, also, to Jamie Turek, for the stunning covers that he has designed for this and my other books.

chapter one

Prelude

It all began when, at the age of 68, I finally found the courage to leave my husband and started backpacking around the world.

Until then I had led a dull and mundane life, manipulated first by my father later by my husband. As frightened as a scared rabbit, I was withdrawn and insular, with no idea of what lay beyond the boundaries of my own little world.

During the seven years following that giant leap into the unknown I visited 46 countries, went to India three times and travelled to Egypt twice.

The story of how I finally came to free myself from the constraints of my marriage I've told in my forthcoming biographical book, *A Journey Beyond The Spirits*. In it I recount how I began to find my inner self and follow my intuition for the first time in my life - things that I had never done before.

The sense of freedom I felt was indescribable. I felt like a bird released from a cage that had suddenly discovered wings! There was so much out there to be seen and waiting to be explored: so many things that I just hadn't known about before.

My next book, *Divine Mystery*, follows my journey through the last four countries that I visited and some of the amazing stories from the many people that I met along the way.

After all this travelling I was guided to Ibiza, where I lived for five years and where I had a strong feeling that I was meant to be.

But before I could finally call the place home, I had to cut my ties to England.

During the seven years that I was travelling the world, I had always maintained a base in England - a caravan that I kept on a site in Sidmouth in Devon. I had bought it immediately after I left my husband. Now it was proving to be something of an obstacle for me to surmount before I could finally pack up my few remaining material possessions and leave England for good.

At that time that I bought it I thought I had a ten-year lease on the caravan. But I had just left my marriage of 47 years and I was in a fairly frantic state of mind. As it turned out I only had an eight-year lease on it. Now, when I wanted to leave after nine years, the owner of the caravan park was demanding a further £2000 for the extra year that I had stayed!

When I asked him how much he would give me to buy the caravan from me, he told me he couldn't say until nearer my time of leaving.

Two weeks before I was due to leave I asked him once again. This time he demanded that I pay him £650 to walk away.

I already knew something about how ruthless this man could be....

He'd given the lady in the caravan next door to me just £400 for her caravan when she'd wanted to leave because her husband had cancer. Then he'd gone on to sell it for £12,000. He'd also told her that she had to pay a year's rent, even though she was not going to be there. She'd gone to a solicitor and won the case in the end, but that awful man had reduced her to tears in the process, with all the diabolical things that he'd said to her. She was not a young woman and she had enough problems with her husband being ill. The man had no compassion whatsoever.

Knowing how hard nosed and callous the man was, I decided I would not pay him any more money. I arranged for someone to buy the caravan for £650, and received a cheque for that amount. But, when I tried to hand that over to the caravan park owner, he refused to accept it and would not let the buyer take *my* caravan. The solicitor we got onto the case told that it wasn't worth carrying on to the bitter end for the small sum of money involved. The caravan park owner was made to pay £450. That was probably nothing to him. He subsequently sold my caravan and very likely got £10,000+ for it.

But, what goes around comes around, and he will get his comeuppance eventually.

I also had difficulty getting my insurance refund from him. Beware people, if you are buying a caravan in England: caravan park owners are a law unto themselves, and you can't do anything about it.

Packing up to leave England was another challenge. I had decided to give up all my material attachments. That turned out to be one of the hardest things I have ever had to do and there were some things I really wanted to keep. In the end, though, I told myself firmly that it was for the best and took only what would fit into four suitcases, two backpacks and a box. Just two days before leaving I sold the car that I had bought only four-and-a-half months previously. Then I spent my last two nights before leaving England on this journey into the unknown at a Bed and Breakfast.

I booked Phil, my usual taxi driver, to drive me to the airport and he kindly helped me in with all my luggage when we arrived there. It was a relief to hand the four cases to the airline attendant and discover that they were not over the extra weight allowance that I had bought online. It had been difficult to stand on the scales at home, holding each one in turn, to estimate the weight. I had been concerned that they would be exceeding the limit.

Finally I was on my way to a new life, after all the extraordinary adventures that I'd had on my journey so far. Now, over the first hurdles of my latest exploit, I could relax and plan the next chapter of my life. My first love in life is to have my hands in the soil. I was looking forward to settling down again to follow my passion for organic gardening. With 20 years' gardening experience, I knew I had a good basis for my new venture – to create a fruit forest founded on permaculture principles. Now I had to learn what I could grow in Ibiza.

It was hard to contain my enthusiasm. This is the story

of that quest.

chapter two

Why Ibiza?

One of the places I had visited during my travels was the Aegean, where I'd explored the Greek islands.

Planning to take the ferry from Piraeus to Mykonos, I'd overslept after a long journey. Rushing to the port, I hastily joined the boat, quickly flashing my ticket as I boarded before settling down for the crossing. Later, when I asked the purser how much longer it would be before we reached Mykonos, he told me I was on the wrong boat! Fortunately I had not booked to stay anywhere, so it didn't matter.

As things turned out, I was on the right boat for the Universe.

The boat was heading for Santorini. On the way we'd stopped at the island of Paros. I'd liked the look of the place and decided to return there after a few days' rest on Santorini.

From Paros I went to the tiny island of Antiparos where I met a woman from Norway. As it was her birthday, I went to a jewellery shop to buy her a present, and met a lovely woman who was selling the jewellery. She was from Ibiza and told me about all the interesting things that were going on in the alternative community on the island. It was she who suggested that I go there.

I didn't take up her offer of going. But eighteen months later I was drawn back to Antiparos and to her. She invited me to join her in a meditation at her house. When I arrived I found a circle of lights and crystals on the floor in the centre of the room. After our meditation we sat chatting over a cup of tea and she asked me again if I would like to go to Ibiza. In the end I agreed that I would go. The following September I found myself there for a four-week stay.

At first I felt depressed and very alone. Then, walking through some small woods one day I stopped. As I listened to the birds and smelt the pine trees the thought entered my head: 'I could live here.' I never thought for a moment that I would actually do so. My intention at that time was to go and live on the Maltese island of Gozo.

I think the thought had been planted in my head to guide me to Ibiza. I did go and spend six months in Gozo, but four-and-a-half months after my first visit to

Ibiza I had moved over, lock, stock, and barrel. There had been no ifs, buts, or maybes about it. I had known intuitively that that was where I needed to be.

It felt like the place that I would put down my roots.

COMING HOME

I had asked my friend Noelia, who comes from the Basque country, to meet me at the airport, knowing that she had a car big enough to hold all of my luggage. She replied that her husband needed the car that day, so she wouldn't be able to help me.

At that I took a deep breath and decided that I would just have to go with the flow and see what would transpire. Then, four days before I was due to leave England I received an email from her telling me that she would have the car that day and could meet me after all.

Once again, I felt the universe was helping me.

Arriving at Ibiza Airport I wondered, as I stood at the conveyor belt waiting for my last remaining worldly possessions, how I was going to gather up all my paraphernalia alone. There were the four cases, the two backpacks - and the lady's spade and garden fork that I had found it impossible to leave behind.

Along came three of the cases, the two rucksacks, and the spade and fork but there was no sign of the fourth case.

After what seemed like an eternity, it emerged – but open, with a broken zip and its contents falling out all over the place. Needless to say this was the most important case, containing as it did my precious Vita-mix and my radio! While I struggled to get it off the belt people all around helped by gathering up my scattered possessions as they rolled away on the conveyor belt.

It must have been quite a comical sight, if I think back to it. Especially when, having shepherded all my belongings together again, I had to cram everything back into the case. There I was, in the middle of the bustling baggage hall, trolleys and flustered travellers all around, stooping over a broken suitcase spilling over with rumpled pillows, sheets and towels. Anxiously I hurriedly tried, as best as possible, to wrap my treasures up again in their protective padding.

Eventually, with the help of a kind fellow passenger I made it to the airport entrance. I was enormously grateful that Noelia was there, waiting to meet me. Together we negotiated the precariously loaded trolley to her car. An overwhelming sense of having come home washed over me as we drove away from the airport. It had been raining in England when I left. Here in Ibiza the sun was shining and the skies were a clear blue. It felt good to be here.

Luckily I was able to return to have my old apartment in Ciel Azul in Cala Martina, near Santa Eulalia. I had stayed there during my first visit to the island four-and-half months earlier. The plants I had put into the wall then looked in a sorry state after all that time of neglect, but with tender loving care and some much needed rain they soon recovered. A trip to the garden nursery with a friend followed and, before long my new collection of flora was helping to make the place more homely. I can't live without plants - they cheer me up so much.

Sorting everything out took a bit of doing, of course, and kept me busy for a while.

Soon after I arrived I met a Mayan Astrologer who told me that, according to the Mayan way, I am red earth and that it was not surprising that I had come to the island. This is because the earth in Ibiza is red. Then I got to thinking and realized that, where I used to live in Sidmouth Devon, there is also red earth. Incredible is it not!

For the first ten months I didn't have a car except for the occasional rental car. To do my shopping I would walk the five kilometres along the coast from Cala Martina to Santa Eulalia and get a taxi back. It felt good to be living in a way more closely aligned to my idea of environmental awareness by not having a car. And it was a beautiful walk that I looked forward to every week.

I would like to have continued living without a car, but that made it difficult to join a walking group that I really wanted to be part of, so in the end I did buy one. For those first ten months, though, I didn't meet many people and lived quite a solitary life.

But I was always being taken care of. That I did know.

Some people may not believe in angels, but I do know that I am well looked after, and one or two people have said they can see angels round me. I keep them around me ever since a friend told me to keep them with me always some years ago.

Once, during my walk into town I tripped and fell forward, but didn't actually go down. I simply kept walking, bent forwards for a few steps, and then slowly came upright. I had the feeling that I was being pulled up by some unseen power. I am sure my angels were helping me. It would have been nasty had I gone down on to the ground in a gravel car park.

You just have to believe in your angels and ask for their help. They are waiting to be asked. They have never let me down.

chapter three

Settling In

'November 2012: The forecast was good for three days so I hired a car to explore the island. It's so quiet at this time of year; so different from the chaotic summer, when three million visitors invade the place. In winter the roads are quiet, the beaches are empty and not many restaurants are open. I just love the winter.'

'The sea was calm. I found a tiny bay, Es Pou des Lleo close to San Carlos, where a fisherman was working on his boat in front of his boathouse edging the beautiful turquoise waters. There are many banks of these quaint little fishermen's boathouses fringing bays and beaches all around the island. They would have played an important economic role in earlier days, when fishing was a major source of food supply, but these days they are mainly kept for recreational purposes

and in high demand despite apparently strict rules as to how they can be used and changed. Usually they are passed from generation to generation.'

Platja Pou des Lleo, I discovered, played a significant role during the Spanish Civil War. On August 8th 1936 Air Force Captain Alberto Bayo led a task force of navy ships — a battleship, two destroyers, four transport ships, a submarine — and six seaplanes, and landed one thousand Republican troops in the bay to re-capture the island from the Nationalists who had taken it at the beginning of the conflict. They had been advised and guided by Republicans from Santa Eulalia.

These days there is no sign of any conflict. The bay is peaceful and surrounded by tranquil wooded hills.

From the bay I walked up a path along the coast and followed a track through pine woods that took me up to a high point and the Torre d'en Valls . The tower is one of the many pirate lookout towers that are all around Ibiza. They were built during the 16th, 17th and 18th centuries to warn the islanders about approaching pirate ships that would make frequent devastating plunerdous raids on the indigineous population.

I decided to climb up it. From the top there were stupendous views across to the island of Tagomago. I later discovered that it belongs to a German man who rents it out during the summer, and charges a fortune for the privilege.

At around that time I made a diary note that read, *'Ibiza is not cheap, but there is something so special about this island. It has very strong energies that keep many people here, though for some people the energies are too strong and they have to leave.'*

The following Sunday I went up to San Juan in the north of the island, to the Sunday market. It is held in the centre of the village, in a cobbled square, surrounded by trees. In November they were decked in bright yellow autumn foliage and dappled in the sunlight. The market had been established only two weeks previously but even in that short time it had already expanded greatly.

There were stalls selling all kinds of organic produce – fruit, vegetables, juices, breads, bio skin creams, jewellery, clothes, and all sorts of handmade crafts. A live band played at lunchtime and created a wonderful atmosphere. People danced in the square and there was even a yoga class going on.

My friend Mary had a stall there, selling second hand things. Mary was a young, single mother of two whom I had met at Ciel Azul. Like so many people that had come to live in Ibiza, she had many skills – as well as playing classical cello she was also a trained osteopath and a very good masseur. I went to her for a weekly massage for a long time. She was very spiritual, and very kind and caring. She introduced me to Toby Clarke, who leads the walking club, Walking Ibiza. This was just what I had been looking for, but sadly it would be another year before I could join the group, when I had bought a car of my own.

After the market Mary, her little two-year old daughter and I drove to Casita Verde on the other side of the island.

Casita Verde is a completely self-sustaining permaculture project that was established in 1996. The house is situated on a hillside with a magnificent view down the valley and on to the sea in the distance. It's a great place to sit under the trees enjoying a vegetarian lunch.

On Sunday afternoons Chris, the owner, gave people a tour of the project that had been evolved to make the best use of the terrain and the available natural resources. Shower, washing machine, and sink were all at the top of a bank so that wastewater could run down the hill to water the fruit trees. Solar energy heated the water for everything. Two eco toilets had been built on top of a wall so that the compost could fall through below. After three months the compost could be used to fertilise trees or shrubs, but was not used on the vegetables. Rainwater collected from the roof was stored in a huge tank for people to use to wash their hands. When the rains were heavy the water that washed down the roads was channelled into a huge tank to provide water through the summer. For cooking they harnessed the sun's energy on a large silver disc that could be rotated to follow the sun's movement across the sky.

There was also an ingenious adobe building made of mud and bottles, with an inverted satellite dish forming part of the roof. Decorating the floor was a beautiful design created from broken tiles by a volunteer artist. Most things on the project had been built using recycled materials.

Volunteers stayed in a Mongolian yurt or an Indian tepee. There was also accommodation in caravans, a cave, a tree house, and a wooden building with wonderful views of the sunset by way of accommodation. In a separate healing area people could have massages.

chapter four

Portal Opening at Tanit's Cave

'Today I rang to book a rental car and the time was 11.11.'

I first met Hilary Carter, author of the *11.11 Code,* in Goa under amazing circumstances. Guided by the number 11, she goes around the world to clear ley lines (also known as energy lines) that have become blocked over the years. She is doing a great job.

She contacted me saying she had work to do opening a portal on Ibiza The portal was at Tanit's Cave near Cala San Vicente and she needed to do the ceremony on 11.11 2012. She asked if she could come and stay with me. Shortly afterwards Ibiza was mentioned on her Facebook Page. She saw that as a definite sign that she needed to come and arranged to come for 11 nights

(we both always follow the signs given to us)

Her visit was marked by a series of strange synchronicities that confirmed our conviction that what she had come to do was aligned with a higher purpose. The first day that we went out together we saw a car with an 1111 number plate. On another day we saw more car number plates with repeating numbers – 222 on one and 444 on another.

We visited my friend Mary who gave Hilary a book to look at and she just happened to open it at a page number that added up to 11. More interestingly, though, it was at a passage recounting an accident involving a lorry that had run into a car. Something just like that had relatively recently happened to Hilary, so she knew that she needed one of Mary's special massages to work on clearing any residual trauma.

We had intended to hire a car to get us there, but then my friend Christine offered to take us in her car and suggested that we take a picnic and make a day of it.

Christine was someone else whom I had met at Ciel Azul. She had very kindly showed me around when I first came to Ibiza. We often walked together – along the coast and through the woods - and became good friends. Together we would regularly go to a swimming pool, the sauna, and a Hammam in Ibiza. I feel a real affinity with her.

On the day of the ceremony at Tanit's Cave we parked the car at the house of a friend of Christine's who then took us to the start of the goddess path up to the mountain and the cave.

We donned our boots and started to climb. There, right at the beginning of our climb, Christine found a lingam and a two-euro coin on the path. Was that a sign, we wondered?

It is a beautiful track with spectacular views down the valley to the sea at Cala Vincente, made even more picturesque in January and February when the almond trees are in blossom filling the landscape with colour and the delicious scent of honey in the air.

How many people must have used this path in the past? How must it have been when there were no roads?

As we climbed higher we visualised leaving our light on the path. We passed a goddess sign and followed the meandering path through pine trees with its understory of heathers and native plants, and the intoxicating smell of Mediterranean air. As we walked we gathered rosemary, heather and sage flowers to put on the altar for our ceremony to open the portal at the cave.

We had arranged to meet our friends Mary, Dominic, Rosa and baby Nalini at the cave. Guess what! Just as we were coming up the mountain they were coming down from the car park! We had all arrived at the same time. What synchronicity!

Hilary arranged the altar with flowers and three sticks of incense. Then, with Hilary leading us, we all stood in a circle holding hands while we brought in the light and opened the portal. After that Hilary began to do the clearing while simultaneously linking with somebody in Canterbury to clear the earth's grid. First she cleared Christine and me and then she cleared an energy line that runs between the cave and Turin.

And all the while that she was clearing I played my Tibetan bowl.

The ceremony lasted an hour then Hilary, Christine and I walked back down the mountain in beautiful sunshine. It seemed as though the sun had come out especially for us between the bouts of rain that fell before and after our ceremony.

Afterwards Christine drove us through the countryside to the lovely bay at Benirrás on the north coast of the island where we picnicked on the deserted beach before heading on to magical Es Vedra further down, south, and west.

The small island of Es Vedra off the west coast of Ibiza is the third magnetic point on the planet after Antarctic and Arctic, and it is a place with very special energies.

As Christine and I stood facing the island Hilary connected with it and then worked on clearing stuff from us energetically. A dramatic clap of thunder ripped through the sky after she had cleared me - just as there had been a clap of thunder after she cleared me in my room at Solstice! Amazing!

It started raining heavily.

Christine walked down the beach to the edge of the sea under her umbrella. In her hand she held the lingam that she had found on the Goddess path. On an impulse to clear something within her, she threw it into the sea and in that instant the sun appeared through the clouds and bathed Christine in a sliver of light. Everywhere else there were dark clouds and rain. It was another magical moment.

After the portal opening there were terrific storms for a couple of hours. Hail covered the car park, gardens, and fields. Rivers appeared everywhere, running down to the beach in deep gullies and washing the sand from the beaches. I think this was a clearing of the earth and fresh protection. When the seaweed, Poseidonia Oceanica is washed up onto the beaches during the winter storms it helps to protect the beaches from erosion of the sands.

Even so, towards the end of November my diary entry reads, '21.11.2012: It's nearly the end of November and Christine and I are still swimming in the sea and doing yoga on the beach in winter sunshine. There's not a soul around.'

chapter five

Things Always Turn Out For The Best

When I left England on October 10th there were a
couple of things that I couldn't fit into my case – some
bath mats and my CD holder. A friend had offered to
send them to me and I had been expecting them for
quite a while. Months later they still hadn't arrived and
I couldn't contact him by email or phone. Somehow I
hadn't yet got around to writing a letter either.

On Saturday 29th December, when I got home after
my walk to Santa Eulalia, I found a card under the door
saying there was a parcel for me. I would have to wait
now as it was New Year and the shops were going to
be shut for several days.

The following Wednesday, 2nd January, I decided to
walk in to Santa Eulalia to do my weekly shop. I had
finally written the letter to my friend asking about my

things and was taking it with me to post. Fleetingly, I wondered if the parcel that was waiting for me was from him. As I collected it from the post office, I also tried to buy stamps for my letter to England only to be told, for some reason, to go and get them from the Tabac shop! Loaded as I was with my shopping and the parcel, I couldn't face the extra bother.

I reached home at 13.13. Imagine my delight when I opened the parcel to find my bath mats and CD holder! I had been thinking I could really do with my mats, as it was so cold on the bathroom floor.

It was just as well I hadn't bothered to buy that stamp. I am always surprised and delighted at the outcome of things.

chapter six

Ibizan Spring

JANUARY 2013

'Today I have walked along the coast. I'm sitting on a rock overlooking the sea, surrounded by the fresh green leaves of bulbs growing in stony ground. There are flower seed heads blowing in the breeze. A cormorant sits patiently on the rocks where the sea is gently swirling the base. There's an egret on another rock. The sun is peeping through clouds. How lucky I am to be here in this magical, peaceful place. I look across the rocky islands to Es Canar with its backdrop of pine-covered hills. It is so serene.'

'Christine and I went for a seven-and-a-half kilometre walk through a valley set between pine woods at Es Broll Forada near San Rafael. Almond blossom was just emerging from its winter sleep against a clear blue sky and the fields were covered with a profusion of yellow *oxalis flowers. We found some clear running water and decided to meditate barefoot on the grassy field in the valley. I am so lucky to be able to do this in winter.'*

While out walking one day I came across a local farmer in a field working in the old ways. He was sitting on the ground and cutting down the vegetation that he then bundled into the back of his car. I tried to ask, in my haltering Spanish, what he was going to use it for. He replied 'BAA'. It was for his sheep!

I used to walk past that field often and found it interesting to keep track of how they would work the land.

Later in the year he ploughed the field with what was left of the vegetation. He made furrows and then walked along them laying potatoes on top. Another man followed behind him and finished planting them.

He also had a field of poppies and peas that he let die back. I couldn't understand this at first but later found out that it's because peas are nitrogen fixers.

SPRING EQUINOX

Friends from Ciel Azul took me to a Shaman ceremony at Es Vedra.

'In a clearing overlooking the offshore island there was

a large circle of many people. Two people were blowing through shells to make music and sacred sage was set alight in a pot filling the air with smoke. The shaman leading the ceremony had a feathered band on her head. A sparrow hawk was gliding in the thermals overhead. We meditated in a circle of stones to the sound of bells - beautiful under a clear blue sky. We were there for at least an hour.'

'Christine took me to San Juan market. There was a music festival out in the open. Stalls selling everything from crystals to plants and tasty organic food lined the edge of the square. There were so many colourful characters. It makes life interesting. Dancing in the late afternoon sun was a delight. A different type of music was played every half hour. There is always something going on in winter in Ibiza. That is what is so lovely about the place.

'RAW FOOD RETREAT

I was invited to a raw food retreat that was being run at the Ciel Azul apartments. I thought it would be interesting to join it.

It was being run by a young man from London called Ladrhyn, who was going to teach us how to follow a raw food diet. Twenty youngsters were attending. Most were from London but there was one girl from

Portugal, a man from Poland and a Russian girl who led early morning yoga classes on the beach each day.

Also giving us instruction were Todd, who talked to us about lucid dreaming and out-of-body experiences, and Graham who was a nutrition expert. Graham was a fund of information about the wild plants that we could eat or use as herbal medicine. Amazingly it turned out that he knew Keith, the Chocolate Shaman in Guatemala whom I had also been to see during my travels around the world.

Back at the retreat the boxes of fruit and vegetables tempted us with their bright colours and glossy skins. There were oranges, red peppers, bananas, courgettes, cucumbers, tomatoes, apples, watermelons, mango, and we could help ourselves to whatever we wanted, whenever we wanted.

During the retreat I learnt about the value of using raw food for good health because they retain the enzymes that are otherwise cooked out. We also learnt how to get the best from the raw foods by making smoothies and fresh salads.

I stayed on raw food, eating fish only once a week, after the retreat and felt so good with lots of energy. I would have kept it up for longer but three months later I went back to England and staying with family and friends made it difficult to keep eating only raw food. Nevertheless, while I was there I did try to get organic food whenever I could.

chapter seven

England

JANUARY 2013

'Noelia and her husband took me to the airport to go to England. Luckily they came in to the building with me because I had got the flight time wrong. My flight had left at 3.15 a.m. I had arrived for a 3.15 p.m. flight.'

I had been telling myself that I did not want to leave the island so I believe this was why I had missed the flight. I decided to say 'I do want to go.' But, when I tried to book another flight everywhere was closed. So my friends kindly took me back to the apartment at Ciel Azul where they allowed me to sleep in the room that I had just vacated for the afternoon.

I phoned Mary to see if I could go and stay with her after that. She very generously came to pick me up and took me back to her apartment. In fact she was kindness itself as, though she had no room for me really, she let me have her daughter's bedroom, then she and her two children slept on the floor until I got a flight five days later. They looked beautiful all sleeping together.

'An excellent friend when I was in need. I helped her with the children that week, as she was going through a bad patch.'

I finally arrived in England on July 4th and stayed with my son and his family for four days before going to visit my lifelong friends, Gill and Mike, for a week.

At the end of my stay, Mike took me to the station to catch a train for Bosham, near Chichester, where I was going to go and stay with my friends David and Betty for a few days.

He was out of the house for just a short time, giving me the lift, and doing some shopping, but it was long enough for the burglars who broke into their house in his absence.

Mike, very aware of the risk of burglars, had double locks on the doors and locks on all the windows, but the burglars just smashed the patio doors to enter the house. Extraordinarily, the neighbours had not heard a thing.

Mike and Gill had several things stolen and were compensated for their losses. I lost my laptop and camera, and had money stolen. Unfortunately I wasn't covered by any insurance and in the end I decided not to get another camera.

There were some strange synchronicities about the whole incident. Thinking back, Gill remembered that they had last been burgled twenty-three years after their marriage. This incident was another twenty-three years later. Then, when we went to visit a friend's house it was number 23!

Angel Number 23 is a reminder that your angels are assisting you with maintaining your faith and trust in the Universe. When you are feeling doubt and fear remember to ask the angels for help and guidance. They are always available to support, guide, and assist you - all you need to do is ask.

At the end of July I took the train to Bath where I was going to meet my friend Jacqueline, who was coming up from Devon to see me.

I took a taxi from Bath Spa Station to the Bed & Breakfast that I had booked through an internet booking company several months previously. I should have known to expect trouble, though, because I didn't receive a reply to my email informing them that I would be coming on 31st July. When I arrived they told me that I had booked for the 30th. They did not have a room for me, they said. My booking was now cancelled because I hadn't turned up on the 30th. I had to pay £85 for the night I had not been there!

Proof of my version of events when I showed them the internet booking was of no avail. I was annoyed and was a bit off with them after that. Luckily they did have one small room vacant, but the price was more than for the room that I had originally booked. It had been a good offer. I did stay there in spite of the disagreement, but I have to say I really didn't feel at ease during my time at the place.

It's all about money. I wonder if they are any the happier for having it.

The place was near a mill house where you could catch a boat to take you to the centre of the city. This was perfect because I wanted to shop for things I couldn't get in Ibiza. Besides, although I had lived in Devon for years I had never been to Bath before. It is such a beautiful city.

'The energies are very high, pulsating through my head. I have a headache and a heavy head, all to do

with ascending. Tomorrow my friend Jacqueline is driving up from Devon to see me.'

The day spent with Jacqueline was a lovely day. I was so excited to see her again. We walked along the river and shared a picnic that she had brought. After not seeing each other for a year we had a lot to talk about – how we had each evolved on our spiritual paths.

EYEBODY RETREAT

After Bath my next port of call was Abergavenny, in Wales, to join the Eyebody Retreat that I had booked. I was going to try and clear my cataracts using natural means, without surgery.

It was something that I had wanted to be able to do, but hadn't known how. I had been on the brink of arranging to have the operation when a chance meeting set me on this new direction.

Somewhere during my travels around the country those few weeks that I had been in England I'd met a lady who'd told me about Eyebody. It's a natural, whole body system for improving all kinds of visual problems, including cataracts, known as the Grunwald Technique.

I had checked the website and had been impressed enough by what I'd read to consider trying the method. Scrolling down the page I'd discovered that Peter Grunwald, the founder of the system, would be running an Eyebody Workshop in the UK. The dates coincided perfectly with my plans. It was to take place during the week before I was going to visit a friend in Wales.

Coincidentally the Workshop venue was also in Wales! And that only happens once a year! Amazing!

With such astonishing synchronicities I felt that I was really meant to go. The dates did overlap with a Vipassana Meditation Retreat that I had previously booked, but I cancelled that now in the light of the way things were evolving.

To get to Abergavenny I took the train again, using tickets that I had booked weeks earlier. It was cheaper that way. And when I arrived there I found myself in the company of several others who were also waiting at the station for the minibus that would take us to the Workshop venue at Buckland Hall.

Buckland Hall is an ancient mansion set in the heart of the Brecon Beacons National Park.

Immaculately kept lawns surround the house. They sweep down a hill where there are the remnants of a once beautiful garden in 60-acre parkland that runs along the River Usk and includes woodlands and an arboretum of specimen trees.

I was surprised by how many of us were attending the Workshop - there were 42 of us.

Peter Grunwald himself was leading the Workshop. This remarkable man has evolved the Eyebody system for improving eyesight. At the core of his work is the principle that vision is largely a brain activity. In order to improve it, states Grunwald, we need to learn to see consciously, and we need to improve our peripheral vision. Over a period of many years he has developed an extraordinary range of activities to help people improve their vision.

On the second night of the retreat we all assembled outside the house and Peter allocated each of us a number. Peter himself was No 1, the leader, and there was a middleman and a back marker.

Working with a partner, we were to walk in the forest, in the dark, without our glasses on, for two-and-a-half hours. Our allocated numbers were to help Peter keep track of us in case we got lost. The idea was to get our eyes accustomed to the dark. We were to walk quietly and with presence, thinking of our higher visual cortex while walking. (The visual cortex is the large area at the back of the brain that is involved in all aspects of vision.)

While we were walking we were to take it in turns to also wear an eye mask. Curiously, when I was wearing mine I felt as if I was walking left, even though I was actually walking straight. At one point we reached a dead end and had to turn back. Then we got into a real muddle, bumping into the others who were coming towards us. It was quite scary in the deep darkness, in the heart of the countryside, away from any artificial or dispersed light. We really could not 'see' anything.

My partner and I tried to keep touching the two people in front of us so that we didn't get lost. When we eventually got out of the woods it took the back marker, number 33, who was a big laugh, ages to shut the gate in the dark.

We were told not to put any lights on once we arrived back at the house, and to end the day by mentally running through the day's events backwards. It all aroused very disturbing feelings and made me feel physically exhausted by the time I went to bed. Despite that, though, neither my room-mate nor I slept very well that night for the strangeness of how we were feeling.

Something else that we did was eye sunning every morning. We would face the sun with our eyes closed and let the light coming through our eyelids 'bathe' our eyes for five minutes. After that we did 'palming' the eyes to rest them. There were also all kinds of physical activities that also exercised our eyes, our minds, and our bodies by keeping us on high alert. One that I remember very vividly was playing ball - only the ball wouldn't come from somewhere obvious; it would suddenly appear from nowhere.

The food was vegan and so delicious that I always looked forward to the next meal.

My eyesight was indeed much better after all the intensive work. There was one lady participant who went to the optician both before and after the retreat to monitor any changes. The sight test confirmed that there had been an improvement in her vision.

I bought myself a set of pinhole glasses, as recommended by Peter, and continued with the work and the exercises after the retreat, and never did need the cataract operation. My eyesight has remained excellent ever since.

It was time to leave Abergavenny. I was on my way to Milford Haven to stay with my good friend Sue, whom I had met in Spain eight years earlier.

The station was very quiet. There was nobody around.

My case was heavy, and I needed to carry it up a set of stairs, over a bridge and down more steps to reach another platform. I asked the Universe for help. Out of the blue a young man on a bicycle appeared from nowhere and offered to carry it across for me.

Thank you Universe.

This happens to me all the time. I ask for things and trust. Then they happen. It's something I've done on all my travels and always received the help I've needed.

MILFORD HAVEN

Sue, her partner, Stuart, and I went to St Govan's Chapel in Pembrokeshire one day during my stay with them.

St Govan's is a tiny chapel tucked away between two cliffs and dates back to at least the 13th century. It may be even older. There may have been a well there once too. To access it you have to go down 52 steps from the top of the cliff. They say that St Govan is buried there. To me the energies of the place felt very high.

We walked along the coast through a profusion of flowers - purple heather and yellow gorse intermixed into a glorious patchwork of colour. Butterflies flitted from flower to flower. The wildlife there was clearly abundant. The truth of the matter is that the area is a Military Training Area and it has never been sprayed with herbicides and pesticides!

It is sad that so many places that used to have a profusion of flowers have been sprayed with poisons that have killed the beautiful flora and, of course, all the beneficial insects too. I was told that there used to be many wild flower fields in Ibiza, until they started to spray with poison. There are still some wild flowers but there is no longer the same great diversity that there once was.

Hopefully, if people go more organic the flowers will return.

Sue, Stuart, and I walked on, enjoying sunshine and wind until we ended up at a long sandy beach. From there we found a path under dappled shade from the trees that led inland to a magical expanse of water surrounded by woods and covered in water lilies – the Lily Pond. It was quite enchanting.

GLASTONBURY

After a wonderful week Sue took me to the station to catch the train to Bristol. From there I was catching a bus to Glastonbury.

I had just settled down in my seat on the bus when a

young man came over to speak to me. At first I was a little taken aback, and then amazed and delighted. It was Graham, whom I had met in April, on the Raw Food Retreat in Ibiza. He too was on his way to Glastonbury, but he had missed the previous bus. Had that not have happened we would never have bumped into each other.

He called it a hyper-magical vortex of synchronicity!

When we arrived he helped me off the bus with my case and took me to meet his friend, who ran a raw chocolate shop. As we chatted I discovered that this friend had once had a raw food restaurant in Santa Gertrudis, right in the heart of the island. Unfortunately he had been a little ahead of his time, had run out of money and hadn't been able to make it pay. Since then raw food restaurants and organic shops have sprung up everywhere in Ibiza.

I had come to Glastonbury to have another Reiki attunement with Valerye. This time it was Anubis Reiki that draws in very powerful energies and clears many spiritual blockages.

Over the years, my contact with Valerye has been singularly marked by many synchronicities that I have chronicled in my previous books.

During my stay in Glastonbury I took a bus to Bridgewater to meet my author friend, Hilary Carter. There she was, walking down the street towards me just as I arrived, just as I had thought would happen. It was so lovely to catch up again.

We decided to stop for a drink at The Old Vicarage Hotel, an ancient hostelry. As we were ordering our drinks Hilary asked about the Hotel's age and we were shown the oldest part of the place, dating from the 13th Century. The girl showing us around explained that they had uncovered a tunnel in the left hand corner of the fireplace that they believed had led to the Castle. Curiously, Hilary had found a tunnel on the same side of the fireplace in the old convent that she had bought in France.

We could certainly feel the energies in the place, standing in that ancient room.

On August 25th, back in Glastonbury, I woke up with the feeling that something special was going to happen. I decided to climb up Glastonbury Tor. Sitting on the Tor wall was a girl doing Tarot readings so I stopped to have a reading with her, then I walked on to the ley lines. There I found three people sitting around a picture of the Star of David with a huge crystal in its centre and more crystals on each of the five corners. After a while the Tarot reader joined us, and then they performed a ceremony to open a portal on the ley line.

Soon after the ceremony had ended my phone went off. I looked at the time. It was 13.31. I wondered what it was telling me because I kept seeing these numbers. I do believe that if I could remember the thought in my head just before seeing such numbers, I would understand the messages better. I think they are telling me that everything is OK.

When I looked it up later I found that Angel Number 31 is an indication from your angels that they are helping you to gain a positive and optimistic outlook and are helping to empower you so that you can walk your chosen path with confidence and grace. The explanation went on to say, 'Be prepared to expand and develop your personal spirituality in new and exciting ways.'

chapter eight

Back in Ibiza

Mary had kindly let me stay in her apartment while she was in England. I myself had had a strong feeling that I was meant to look after it.

There was a lovely Argentinian lady, Lisi, also staying there. She was setting up an alternative school on Ibiza and had been sharing Mary's place with her before I left for England. We both stayed on at Mary's for the next six months, and then she moved out with me to come and share my new home for another two months when we left.

While I was staying at Mary's place I rented her car from her, but it was a mixed blessing.

In my diary I wrote: *'I have been renting Mary's car. The door handle came off, so a trip to the garage to have it put right was the order of the day. Then the*

door would not close. That happened at 3.30 a.m., an
unusually late time for me to be going home, and not a
good time for finding help but I was lucky, as usual, and
someone appeared to lend me a hand.'

'After having that put right I had a flat tyre at the front.
A young man at the Rent-a--Car opposite the
apartment helped me with that, pumping the tyre up
so that I could get to a garage. He told me that the
front tyres were illegal. (I think that was the reason
that I had a flat tyre - to alert me to the fact). I had two
new tyres put on.'

Nevertheless, having the use of a car did mean that I
could explore the island more. During one of my
wanderings I found a beautiful restaurant in a tiny inlet
at Cala Mastella. There was a boat tied up at the jetty
and it all reminded me of Cornwall. El Bigotes was the
name of the place and on the set menu they had
nothing but a selection of fish caught that very day.

It was an idyllic place to eat - but very expensive. I was
lucky enough to be taken there as a treat later on in
the year by my friend Gill and another friend of hers,
Daphne.

So many things kept going wrong with Mary's car that I
decided to buy my own. The car hire companies sold
their cars off at the end of the season and I decided

that that would be my easiest option as they arranged all the necessary paperwork. I was having difficulty with the language.

I told the man at Union Rent A Car that I wanted a blue Fiat Panda with a number plate that added up to eleven! The news came back that they did have exactly what I wanted and that I could collect it in three weeks' time.

In the meantime I had go to the police station to get my NIE number. On Ibiza it is not possible to buy a car without one. The form I had filled in had number 11 on it.

I waited for two hours in a separate room, away from all the others that were in the queue. I didn't know why I had been put there and my Spanish wasn't good enough to ask anyone, so I was feeling quite uneasy.

I asked the angels if I could be seen soon. No sooner had I asked than a policeman took me to sit outside, opposite the desks where we were to be seen. He spoke to the man behind the desk issuing the numbers. And so I was the next person to be called, even though there were other people there before me. I was now facing the same man who had told me at first that he couldn't serve me. Clearly the angels were at work.

As I left the police station Christine phoned me. I looked at the phone. The time was 11.11!

Once more I felt blessed.

After yet another problem with Mary's car I decided that I'd had enough of it, so I went back to Union-Rent-A-Car and asked if I could have my car earlier than arranged. They told me that it was still out on hire at that time, but they called the company in Ibiza to see if anything could be done. By chance the man who had hired the car just happened to be in the Ibiza office when the call went through. Better still, he was willing to change the car, so I could have it early.

As if by magic, everything had fallen into place after just three or four phone calls. Before I knew it I had my own car with a two-year ITV (the local road worthiness test) and all the paperwork sorted.

chapter nine

2013 Draws to a Close

October: *'The weather has been fabulous with blue skies most days and very warm. I've had the patio doors open at night and can hear the waves on the shoreline...........'* Then, later that month *'It is the end of October and we are having big storms and torrential rain - much needed.'*

November 10th: *'I walked along the beach at Cala Nova and through woods to the Sunday Market in Cala Llenya. On the way I passed some Spanish women setting up a table ready for lunch in the sunshine. The men were there with their fishing rods, trying to catch fish for lunch. I didn't see them catch anything - fish stocks around Ibiza are depleted, like everywhere else. Nevertheless, it was a lovely sight to behold - they still carry on their traditions.'*

FRANCE WITH CHRISTINE

The day after that entry, on 11th November I flew to Barcelona with Christine. We were en route for a road trip to France.

When we went to pick up the hire car we were told we could not pay by cash, so Christine had to go to pay at a bank. Unbelievable! It's all a ploy by the powers that be to make us reliant on cards, to control us by not letting us use cash. I don't use bankcards unless I really have to.

Driving along the motorway from Barcelona towards the border with France we saw something huge, really huge, there in the sky in front of us. It looked like a cloud with something that looked like a feather on the right side. The bottom of it was grey, the top white. We were sure it was a spaceship, hiding in the clouds. It did not move or change in any way for the entire hour that we were driving. I have since seen a report of another similar one posted on the internet, so am pretty sure it was a spaceship.

When we needed a break from the driving we decided to leave the motorway at a sign to San Christina, near Lloret de Mar. It seemed appropriate to go there, as it was Christine's namesake! There we found a small, deserted bay with huge waves, so we stripped down to the nude and plunged into the heaving waters. It was so invigorating after the long journey. After we had dried off and rested a while, we set off again.

We were heading for Canet de Roussillon, near Perpignan, where Christine had booked an apartment, a choice that had been guided by a hefty 60% reduction on the price. Other holistic venues in the mountains that we had looked at and tried to book had all been very expensive.

Unbeknown to me when we had left Ibiza, this was close to the place where I had spent the last holiday with my husband Gordon before I left him. That had been a very fraught time so I believe I was meant to go there to clear something. We could have gone anywhere in France, but something must have been drawing us to this place. Of all the places that we had tried to book, this was the only place that could take us. It was amazing and seemed to be more than a mere coincidence.

One of the purposes of the trip had been so that Christine could go and visit her grandmother, whom she had not seen for fifteen years. The old lady was staying in an old people's home nearby. And now there was another extraordinary synchronicity. As she entered the building on the day that she went to pay the visit, Christine came face to face with her aunt, someone else that she had also not seen for fifteen years.

The next day we drove to see a sight recommended by the tourist board, the rock formations at Ille Sur Tête. When we arrived we discovered that, officially, the site was closed. But we had driven a long way to get there so we decided to try and find a way in anyway. There was a long walk up a lane through countryside for sometime before we reached the gated entrance to the site. We slid underneath it to go and have a quick look around.

The rocks are formed in the shape of a church organ and are known as the 'orgues'. They form a kind of natural amphitheatre made of tall pillars of sandy white rock that has been eroded into wonderful 'organ-pipe like' shapes up to 12 metres high. Apparently, according to the Tourist Board, when the wind blows you can hear music. It was windy the day we went but we didn't hear anything. All the same, it was quite a sight.

Afterwards we took a road through the mountains, the Pyrenees des Catalanes. I just love the high mountains. We wanted to get to Prades and then on to some sulphur pools at St George. It was a very cold day. We noticed that the cars coming from the opposite direction were covered in snow. Nevertheless, we

drove on up higher into the mountains, into the snow
that kept falling and didn't stop all the way to St
George.

The mountains all around the sulphur pools were
covered in snow. The pools themselves were out in the
open. We looked at each other for a moment and must
have had the same thought at the same time. We had
driven so far to get there that we would go in
regardless of the weather. We hired costumes and
towels and slipped into the warm sulphur waters. It
was magical sitting in the pool, gazing at the feathered,
evergreen trees draped in snow, a yellow leafed tree
gleaming brilliant beside them.

We got out reluctantly when it eventually started to
snow very heavily. In the café they kindly filled our
flasks and bottles with the delicious mountain water
that we enjoyed for quite a few days afterwards. We
also discovered that we had been extremely lucky to
be able to bathe in the waters that Friday. They were
closing for winter on the following Sunday.

Back in Canet de Roussillon we had four days of
horrendous wind and rain. It was so strong that it
literally blew me along the sea front. We sat it out by
letting ourselves be pampered in the hotel with
massages and swimming in the heated, indoor pool.

I think that what we were experiencing was the distant effect of the devastating cyclone, Cleopatra, that hit Sardinia on the 17th and 18th of November and caused massive damage there, killing 18 people and leaving thousands homeless. I read that even as far away as Rome people were affected.

By the time we left it was sunny and clear again and we had a lovely drive over the mountains back to Spain, where it was a lot warmer. On the way we drove off the main road and stopped in a little lane close to some woods to picnic on delicious bread, cheese and juicy tomatoes in the pretty countryside. As Christine had had a sleepless night the night before she rested for a while before we drove on.

Thankfully we reached Barcelona airport just as it was getting dark. The young man who checked our rental car when we returned it said he would close his eyes to a mark that had appeared on the back. We didn't know how it had got there, but we were grateful for the help, feeling blessed once again.

I was invited to Christmas lunch at Ciel Azul along with several other people who were living there. Everybody brought a present. All the presents were numbered and we each drew a number out of a hat for our gift. I drew number 11! I'd drawn 11 the previous year too! One of the guys there at the gathering was surprised, but I wasn't. I felt the angels were giving me another message, reassuring me again that all would be well and that they were looking after me.

DOING IT MY WAY

As the year drew to an end and a New Year dawned I took time to think about my life so far. I wrote:

'This is a very interesting extract from Nancy Detweiler that I thought would be worth thinking about as the year ends and a new one begins.'

'I Did it My Way' *by Nancy Detweiler*

Thinking of the life I have lived for seventy-six years as an Aquarian out of the box, puzzling people, worrying family and friends, refusing to settle into a routine, 8 - 5 kind of life…. As I look back, I consider myself to be one of the richest individuals on the planet! So many people, so many places, so many tears, so many times of rejoicing, so many times of feeling personal fulfilment. My bucket of 'things to do' is empty. I've done everything I dreamed of doing. Had I not done it my way, my bucket would very likely be at least half full.

Give yourself the same gift! BE WHO YOU ARE.

'This is just what I allowed myself to become when I left my husband.'

'I am an Aquarian and I finally let myself be who I am. I travelled the world. I swam with dolphins, sea lions, turtles, a small whale surrounded by a ball of fish. So pleased I did it all. Now I have settled, in Ibiza.'

'Now I have a car. It opens new horizons. I can join the walking club - an opportunity to meet loving, caring, interesting people and explore parts of the island that I did not know existed. Views of outstanding beauty abound, on this paradise island with its turquoise sea and its host of almond blossom trees in January.'

chapter ten

A New Year Dawns

RED RICE DETOX

On Saturday 1st J anuary 2014, as I was walking along the coast in the morning, I received a phone call from my friend Aaron.

It was 11:00!

He was calling to invite me to join a red rice detox week at half price, near San Jose. It was starting at 6.00 that evening. I like to go with the flow and, besides, I felt that I was meant to go. It did not take me long to cancel any appointments that I had booked for the week and throw some clothes into a suitcase.

The retreat was being held in a beautiful large house surrounded by gardens overlooking a view of pine-clad hills leading down to the sea. There were people from every corner of the globe – Panama, Holland, Spain, Japan, Ireland, England.

The whole atmosphere of the retreat was one of quiet mindfulness. The slow, unhurried tea ceremony shown to us by a Japanese lady called Toki reminded us to take more time doing things with more deliberation and consciousness.

Aaron held Chi Gong classes that gave us a chance to practice careful, graceful, conscious movement.

There was a day of silence. I really enjoyed being with myself, away from all the hustle and bustle of daily life.

On another day a local man took us for a walk along the coast from Es Vedra to the beach at Cala d'Hort. When we returned, we climbed down a steep cliff to find a well of delicious sweet water. What a treat that was! After that we went to sit on the cliff top overlooking Es Vedra and watched the setting sun. It was another magical day.

There was a walk one day at Santa Inés through trees in full bloom of almond blossom, when we stopped to sit in a field of lemon yellow oxalis relishing a drink of cool water. They were such simple pleasures that made for a beautiful day.

There were days when we had time to have a treatment or rest in the afternoon. In the evenings there would be a large log fire in a candlelit room, creating a lovely atmosphere.

On the last evening we were all asked to give some kind of presentation to everyone. Someone played guitar and sang. The two Columbian girls got up and danced and urged us all to get up and join in.

Somehow I also found the courage to get up and speak to the group even though this is something that I have always found it difficult to do.

At the end of the retreat Alliwalu, who was running the course, suggested that I have some speech therapy to help me with my fear of public speaking.

She suggested a therapist who could help me and after the retreat I attended speech therapy classes for eight weeks. There were six of us in the class. We were given the task of practising a poem so that we could recite it in front of an audience. Clare, the teacher, had selected a poem for each of us to work on for a final presentation in public at the end of the course.

WHEN I AM AN OLD WOMAN

The poem that she chose for me, even though she had never met me before, was very apt because I mostly wear purple.

On the day of the performance she gave us speech exercises and instructed us on how to breathe beforehand to keep us calm. When it was my turn I amazed myself. I was not at all nervous in front of the big audience that had come to hear us. Doing the course had given me so much more confidence.

This is the poem that I had to read:

When I am old I shall wear purple with a red hat which doesn't go and doesn't suit me

And I will spend my pension on brandy and summer gloves and satin sandals

And say we have no money for butter

I shall sit down on the pavement when I am tired

And gobble up samples in shops

And press alarm bells and run my stick along public railings,

And make up for the sobriety of my youth

I shall go out in my slippers in the rain and pick flowers in other people's gardens

And learn to spit

You can wear terrible shirts and grow more fat and eat three pounds of sausages at a go

Or only eat bread and pickle for a week

And hoard pens and pencils and beermats and things in boxes

But now we must have clothes that keep us dry

And pay our rent and not swear in the street

And set a good example for the children

We must have friends to dinner and read the papers

But maybe I ought to practise a little now?

So that people who know me are not too shocked and surprised when I am old

And start to wear purple

chapter eleven

A House in the Campo

Everybody had told me that I would not find the house and land that I wanted. It's a small island and, with so many people wanting to come and live here from abroad, the demand for housing is very high. I did not listen to them. I just trusted that it would come to me when the time was right.

Then one day I saw a car in San Carlos with a 9999 number plate. In Angel Number Wisdom the number 9 means the completion of a particular cycle of events.

I had always felt that I would find somewhere when Mary came back from England. I had been tentatively looking for a house in the campo (the word here for the countryside) all the time she was away. Now there were only ten days until she came back and I could feel myself beginning to lose faith and not trust.

I had looked at a small caravan to rent on some land that I could use for permaculture, but it was not what I wanted. Just thinking of living on the island in a small caravan made my heart sink and reduced me to tears.

Then, during one of the group walks, I met a lady who rented houses. I gave her my card in the hope that she would be able to help me find somewhere. I found out later that she had lost it but nevertheless she did manage to track me down. She took me to see a house where I would be able to use the land and could make a garden.

Now, suddenly, at the last minute the house had materialised. Everything went through very quickly and I was able to move in on 3rd of March 2014. Before I did so though, I did check that I would be permitted to make myself self-sustainable and have solar energy. I thought the landlord agreed readily.

I loved the house and the area. It was just the right time for planting and I got started, enthusiastically, as soon as I had moved in. The first thing I did, though was to clean the earth using a crystal that had been energised with a magnet.

One of the things that I had done together with Lisl

while we were both living at Mary's apartment was to buy a compost maker. It meant that we could turn all our fruit and vegetable waste into nourishment for the soil instead of packing it into plastic and sending it to the landfill sites.

I had been saving all that compost and now it provided an excellent base for the many fruit trees and bushes that I was planting. It was a joy to me to plant vegetable varieties that I had never grown before – pumpkins, melons, watermelons – and to watch them growing ever bigger and juicier.

By the end of the season I was able to crop enough food to last until the end of March

Curiously, at the end of that March I had an accident. At the time I was working very hard collecting seaweed to feed the soil, going out three times to fill the car to full capacity. Afterwards I was mulching the garden with it. It was all quite tiring. Of course, after the accident, without a car, I could not do that any more for five weeks. I think the accident was a lesson that I was doing too much.

On the 28th March my diary entry reads: *'I had a car accident after walking ten kilometres and climbing the highest mountain in Ibiza, and having lunch. I did not feel particularly tired but it was a long journey home. I was nearly there when I had the accident. I was very lucky, as I only suffered from shock and so did the other girl involved. Luckily she could speak good English and filled in all the forms for me. When the police came they asked me for my driving licence. I did not have it as inadvertently had left it in my other bag. He then asked for my NIE number and said I should always carry my licence. I think the angels were looking after me as usually you get a fine if you drive without ID.'*

I was without my car for two months. Fortunately a bus to Ibiza town stopped at the end of my road and there was a shop nearby that I could walk to. Friends were also very helpful to me – busy people I hadn't even known for long. I was so grateful for their selfless kindness and generosity, and climbed another steep learning curve that taught me about the goodness of people. But after three weeks I did decide to hire a car until I got my own back from the repair.

I had felt so calm at the end of the last retreat that I had been on, but the car accident really knocked me back. I felt now that I really needed rebalancing again. So in April I went on another detox retreat week in a big house called Sunset Mountain, inland from San Antonio. This time it was juices.

When I got there I wrote, *'It is such a release not having the internet or phone. Just being myself. The weather is good this time and we are able to swim in the pool overlooking pine-covered hills to a most beautiful sunset reflecting in the pool. This time the people are mainly from Holland.'*

And later I continued: *'Today was a day of silence, which I really enjoy. We just spent the day being ourselves, meditating, being aware of what we were drinking in our juices, feeling gratitude for the people who make them with pure love, feeling relaxed in our body, content at leaving the material world behind.'*

'In the afternoon we went to Es Vedra and walked along the coast to a beach and some of us swam in the sea. When we arrived back at Es Vedra we climbed down the cliff to watch a fabulous sunset. The sea was so calm. The sun was casting diamonds sparkling on the sea. The sea was infused with pink, with reflections of the clouds. What a wonderful inspiring day we all had. What a great job everybody does to make this all happen - people putting real love into the food we eat and into the massages and the love of the people. This is something I really needed after the accident.'

Another day I wrote: *'It is such a joy to see a long wall of huge rocks in the garden, covered in purple, pink and orange flowers covered in bees. There is also a very unusual shrub by my room with orange flowers covered everyday with bumblebees I need to find out what it is to put in my garden.'*

Then: *'Marta did yoga today with couples. Never done this before. First we sat back to back to feel each other's energies: one of us crouched in the child pose while the other leant backwards over the crouching partner. It loosens the spine. And we held hands in order to help each other stretch different parts of the body. It was very pleasant.'*

One evening Abigail, an English doctor who was a Spinal Balancing Practitioner came to give taster sessions. That night, after my mini-treatment with her I slept like a log from 10 until 7. I was so impressed by the treatment that I started a series of sessions with her after the retreat.

By the end of the week I felt very happy and relaxed and ready to start anew.

I was particularly pleased that Juan was also offering treatments during the retreat. I had had some treatment with him during a previous retreat, so I was happy that I would be able to see him again. It really felt that I needed some help after the accident.

Juan works with magnets. He starts by holding your feet and letting your body tell him where it needs help. Then he corrects the problem by placing magnets on the affected parts. As soon as he held my feet he told me that I had had a shock. Of course it was the accident.

Magnetic therapy is a wonderful concept that people are not aware of and that many are sceptical of, but there is plenty of evidence to show that it works.

People with new healing devices have such difficulty countering the large corporations and prejudices. People are so conditioned to believe that they need to take pills or have operations in order to get well again. It's all just to line the pockets of big business! One Australian doctor told me that cataract operations bring in more money than any other operation and yet they can be cured without – I am living proof of that.

I have a friend who does Scio. This is a bio-resonance technique that gives the practitioner a precise review of biological reactivity in the body. Designed on the principles of Quantum Physics, it is able to diagnose problems through revealing the energetic status of the body. On the basis of that information the practitioner can introduce proper frequency oscillations to bring about a return to homeostasis, or balance.

It is a technique that definitely works and yet my friend has so many problems promoting it. She also uses lasers to cure hip problems so that people can avoid having an operation. She told me how one of her clients with a bad hip came hobbling in with sticks and left without them. On the other hand I have two friends who need hip surgery and who don't even want to talk about the possibility of alternative treatment, let alone look into laser treatment.

chapter twelve

Breath Week

MAY 2014

'May 27th: Today I am joining a group of young people from Holland for a week of breath work. This is a form of clearing out our anger, blocks and traumas.'

We breathed with our mouths open following a set rhythm, first inhaling fresh oxygen and then letting the air out again. While we were breathing Tom, the teacher, came round to each of us in turn and pressed on certain points on our bodies, places where we store our anger. As he pressed we had to exhale and voice loudly at the same time.

When I wrote about it in my journal, I said, *'It is excruciatingly painful, but we have to breathe into our pain and clear it. It's amazing all the parts of our body*

that anger is stored - neck, chest, abdomen, spine.
Then the pain is massaged, the parts of the body are
tapped with fingers. We breathe it out then we have to
tone (a loud "AAH!") to clear the pain. We work for two
hours doing this special breathing. At the end we relax
and are very calm. Each time we breathe, we make an
intention to clear something from our body.'

One afternoon we went to Portinatx to a place
overlooking the sea on the cliffs, where we did some
breathing with the sea pounding below. Two days later
we worked with partners, learning how to interact
without confrontation. We learnt to ask how we felt
when we said certain things to each other and to check
what our needs were at that moment.

On the Saturday we all went to Es Vedra, that very
special place where, if you ask for something while you
are there it often comes to fruition.

It started to rain on our way there. Jay told us about a
deep cave overlooking the island where there's a man
living sometimes. Because of the rain Jay suggested
that we did our breath work there so when we arrived
we climbed down the cliff to find the cave. It was
magical to look out of the cave to see Es Vedra
swathed in the mist rising out of the sea.

There was enough room inside for the six of us -

Amelia, Martin, Carla, Saskia, Jay, and me - to lie down. We had to make our intention then exhale and imagine all the anger flowing out of our bodies with the breath. I imagined it flowing into the sea. Afterwards when I had done the work I lay down and relaxed. I had an extraordinary feeling, as if I was not in my body. All I could feel was the heartbeat of Martin's dog lying beside me.

Amelia had an amazing experience, where she felt that her heart suddenly opened. She said it felt as if everything came up from her hips and poured out of her left ear. Afterwards she felt light and floating and yet grounded at the same time. She wanted to process what had happened but we had to leave to go to a restaurant. When we arrived there she said it was as if she was looking at an illusion, like watching a movie. She had to convince herself that it was reality.

The fish restaurant was perched on the cliffs looking across the bay. The sun was peeping through the clouds and an overhanging cloud shrouded Es Vedra. With the sun lighting it from behind we could clearly see the rocky outline shaped like a lady lying down. Then a rainbow appeared. It made a magical scene and the evening ended with a dinner enjoyed with a group of lovely people. It was quite amazing.

Overall it was quite an intensive week. At one stage,

when I was talking about the problems I was having with the owner of my house at Balafia, one of the things that Tom said to me was: 'Don't get too attached to that house.' It was a prescient comment as I was to discover before too long.

MARTIN AND AMELIA

Martin and Amelia were also participants of the Breath week. They were doing the cooking – raw food and natural juices - in return for being on the retreat. After the morning breath work one day I asked them how they came to be on the island.

Yoga Ibiza had wanted someone to cook for seventy people for five days at Chirincana Restaurant on the beach at Cala Martina where there were diving courses and wind surfing. Amelia and Martin volunteered to work in the kitchen, and were able to live on the campsite for free in exchange. It was there that they met Tom.

Tom was running the Breath Week at Can Salvador. After the week working at Chirincana he invited them to a party at Can Salvador. He was living there and wanted to install a compost toilet. He asked Martin to build them one. It was after that that he and Amelia were invited to the breath week.

This is the way things happen on this island – it's all about networking and going with the flow.

When it was time for Martin and Amelia to leave the community at Can Salvador Tom took them to an isolated and derelict house that he had seen in the mountains. It was difficult to get to as there were trees strewn across the road all the way down to the house. It was in a beautiful valley but nobody had lived there for ten years.

They looked inside. The whole place was full of rubbish. Strewn all across the floor there were pieces of wood and what was left of the owner's belongings. But they could see the potential of the place.

While her friends were looking around the house Amelia walked down to the bottom of the valley. As she stood looking at the view, she looked up into a tree she saw an owl. It flew across in front of her and down the valley. It is very unusual to see an owl in daylight. Amelia thought it was a sign because the owl was Amelia's mascot bird.

It had been her dream to create a retreat. Now she wanted to do it in this valley. She also wanted to grow organic vegetables, and develop her interest in Ayurvedic medicine that both she and Martin were into.

It was a mammoth job for Martin and Amelia to clear all the land. They set to with a friend who came and helped to clear some of the area. In spite of their efforts the road was still blocked, so everything they needed to bring in had to be carried down. Inside they worked hard to put the derelict house into some sort of order, even though they had no electricity.

For a while they squatted undisturbed in the house. Then one day, not long after they had been there, the owner came by. When he saw what Amelia and Martin were doing he told them they could rent it for three years for €200 a month in return for all their hard work in bringing it back into a habitable state.

A little while after they had moved in a friend and I went to visit them to see their place and what they had been doing there. It was quite an adventure to get to the house, and we had difficulty finding it. It was nestled in the bottom of the valley, surrounded by trees though all around the landscape was scarred from a fire that had raged through it ten years earlier. We walked down the gravel road where deep gullies had been gouged out by the rain, and clambering over fallen trees. At one point we even had to scramble down the bank and up again on to the road to get past one. As we neared the house we saw smoke coming from the chimney.

They greeted us warmly when we finally reached the house. A small fire was in the grate where a pot of water was ready to make us a lovely spicy tea. There was nothing much in the house except some cushions on the floor to sit on. The room was spacious, with very high ceilings. The fire was on one side of the room, a small sink unit on the other and there was a little cupboard on the wall. That was it. There were two other rooms downstairs, and in one of them there was a beautiful carved cupboard. Their lovely dog was sitting on cushions. She was due to give birth to puppies any day now.

Climbing the stairs we saw two other bedrooms. One was quite bare and in the other was an old bed with a magnificent carved headboard and a metal base. I wondered if that headboard had been carved by the grandfather that Amelia told us had once lived there. Apparently he had been a wizard and known secrets about nature that nobody else knew.

To get onto the roof we had to climb wooden steps and pass through a very small hole - they must have been very small people in the old days! The views along the valley were awesome. Amelia told us that she and Martin were sleeping on the roof because the house was so full of mosquitoes.

She described her vision of creating a natural healing

centre - a sanctuary where people could be in intense direct healing communication with nature, with a sweat lodge and yoga. She wanted to create a medicinal garden and learn how to heal naturally, with herbs.

After our tea we went to explore the valley. There were many fruit trees and a date palm, and there were areas at the bottom of the valley where it looked as if there could be water. It was a haven for wildlife and a truly peaceful place for relaxing and healing. Amelia's vision included putting up tepees down in that valley for visitors.

Back at the house, she showed me how she washed up and how they showered - using a plastic bottle with a perforated top so that she could squirt water out: not really an ideal shower!

The water in the well was contaminated with dead lizards so they couldn't really use it. Martin was going to have to climb down the shaft to clean in out, a mammoth job. Then the water would have to be pulled up by bucket. For now they had to carry drinking water down to the house from the car at the top of the mountain road. I admired them for being willing to live that way in order to follow their dream.

After a few weeks they got somebody to clear the road

of trees so that they could have easier access.

Soon after that the owner told them to leave. It is a story that I heard over and over again - so many people on the island wanting to do good, then being thwarted by unscrupulous people like that landlord - landlords who offered low rent or long tenancy in return for their work who ultimately turned around and told them to leave.

So Martin and Amelia's dreams were shattered.

chapter thirteen

My Garden In The Campo

That year, back in my garden in Balafia, I learnt a lot about growing in the heat of summer – about offering shade to fruits and vegetables such as celery, beans, courgettes, blackcurrant. I learnt how mulching helps the soil to hold water and how it keeps the fierce sun off the roots of plants.

I also made sure to include an area of plants that would attract bees, butterflies, and other insects.

This was one diary entry from that time: *'I am collecting carob beans from around here. They are excellent for a mulch. I hope to be able to put them through a shredder. Organic coffee beans are a good fertiliser. The owner of the coffee shop at Tetra, just down the San Juan Road has offered me as many dregs as I need for my land. I have had some disasters with my sweet corn. I bought quite big plants - it was so difficult to find organic sweetcorn. The plants were fine. I watered them every day and then, suddenly, they started to die. I looked on the internet and discovered that the seed should be planted in the ground. You cannot put them in a pot. This was a learning curve for me. I found that celery wants a lot of water, and does not like full sun - also cucumbers and dwarf bean. So, next year I will have a pergola built and grow a grapevine up it to shade the vegetables that don't like too much sun.'*

I also went out collecting local seaweed, Posedonia Oceanica, to use as mulch. It rots down very slowly so lasts for a long time, and it feeds the soil at the same time. I always made an effort to collect the old stuff that had been rained on a few times so that some of the salt had been washed out. It was a great success in some places.

That garden was a big project and I couldn't do it all by myself, so I asked the Universe to send me a man to help me. It was going to be heavy work, weeding, clearing, digging, and landscaping that dirty, dusty, rocky plot.

The Universe provided.

Catherine told me about a young man called Vincent. He needed some work for a few weeks before going to work England.

When he left I wrote in my diary: *'Vincent has gone back to England to work so I have lost my help, but the universe was not long in sending me someone else.'*

It sent me Bira.

I had an email from someone I didn't know, telling me that a Canadian lady had recommended him to meet me. She was someone that I had met whilst on a group walk. The man's name was Bira and he invited me to go and see his permaculture plot in the woods close to Santa Gertrudis. Later he very kindly helped me to get horse manure from the stables near him. So I asked him if he would like to do some work for me. He was over the moon about it as he had little work at the time and wanted to save for a trip to India to go on a yoga course. I had only just asked the universe for help - how quickly it comes. He loved working in the garden, talked to the plants and treated them with love, just as Vincent and I did.

Both Vincent and Bira worked very hard to transform that barren, stony space full of buried rubbish into a beautiful garden.

Bira was such a hard worker. I was blessed to have him working for me, and he had such an interesting tale to tell.

BIRA

Bira was Brazilian. For four years he had lived in the rain forest with a particular Shaman community. It was one that he had chosen carefully, after contacting several different ones. He chose that particular one because he liked the seventy five year old Master Shaman, a man strong in presence, in mind and in spirit.

The people of the community were simple, humble people. They were hard workers, strong-minded and very poor, but they had no mortgage so they had freedom. There was a mixture of people – some of African descent, some indigenous, some Caboclo. The Caboclo is a people of mixed Brazilian and European descent, with the word Caboclo being derived from the Portuguese meaning 'copper-coloured'.

They lived a simple life. They did jungle farming, grew fruit and vegetables, built their own houses. They prepared the ground using their own compost and putting down no poison. They had a plant nursery, and for shading they would use palm leaves. They used anything they could find.

Their houses were built of wood from the forest. They would go into the forest to look for dead trees to cut up for their houses then carry the wood as far as four kilometres just to build one house. To get water they had to walk down a hill to the well. Then they would have to carry the heavy 20 litres back up to the community.

They spent a lot of time praying. The women cooked and washed the dishes, the men did hard manual work. Bira would get up at 6 every morning to feed the chickens, collect the eggs and water the vegetable garden before a breakfast of couscous with fried egg and meat.

All the time he was there he wore only flip-flops. One day, when he was walking through the forest he caught sight of what he thought was a tree trunk on the path. On closer inspection he saw it was a huge snake. Luckily it slithered off into the undergrowth when he looked at it.

The community was seventy kilometres from the city and twenty-five kilometres from the nearest village. They did have a community car that Bira would sometimes use to go into town, but at least once a month he would hitch a lift to go for a coke!

GOING GREEN IN THE CAMPO

Throughout the summer and autumn of 2014 I threw all my energies into settling into the house and garden in the campo. I was creating the ecological home that I had so long dreamed about in a place that seemed to be offering me everything I had wished for.

On July 28th my diary entry reads, *'Today I am sitting outside my rustic house under an ancient carob tree listening to the crickets. A parrot in the house opposite is laughing. He takes off the children arguing. Really funny! The swallows are flying in the thermals. So idyllic here.'*

'I will be sorry when my tomatoes are finished - they taste awesome. The taste is totally different from the GMO foods that have no flavour. I don't think I can go back to shop tomatoes. I have just been told that there is a special variety that will keep all winter - a certain type that you pick off the trusses and hang on olive branches through the cold months. I will try this.'

One of the things I wanted to install was a compost toilet. Mary's ex-partner, Domenico, came to make it for me.

We went to buy recycled wood to build a framed box that would hold a five-gallon bucket that could be easily emptied into a compost bin. On top of the box we fixed a toilet seat. The roof of the toilet was sloped so as to feed the rainwater into a reservoir tank that would provide water for washing hands.

Martin had seen a large container on a dump that he thought could be used to hold the collected rainwater. When we went to get it and saw how huge it was we were faced with the problem of how to transport it with only my small Fiat Panda as transport. Then Martin had the ingenious idea of resting a piece of wood against the car so that we could slide it up onto the roof. We fastened it firmly with ropes and so managed to get it back to my home.

It had had some sort of industrial oil in it and smelt terrible. Undeterred, Martin set to. He cut the top off, climbed inside it, and cleaned it out. Then he put vinegar in to take away the awful smell. Before long it was set up and nearly filled with water - probably enough for the summer.

True to my philosophy of trying to re-cycle as much as possible I made a washbasin for the eco-toilet from an old washing machine glass door that I had picked up at the Sunday Market in Cala Lleña. I even found a second hand mirror to put over the washbasin!

Christo from the Permaculture Centre at Casita Verde

came to stay for three nights to show me how to make natural compost. He told me how nature provides everything you need for growing, and collected up soil from round the carob and olive trees to use. He also gathered olive and carob leaves to layer into the compost.

Then he showed me how, by collecting pieces of old wood with fungus on it, I could line the bottom of a raised bed before adding the soil. The rotten wood helps to hold the moisture and the fungus helps to feed the soil.

SACRED DANCE

In July that summer I went to a sacred dance at Solara's Retreat Centre. There was a shaded platform that she had erected for things like this. In the centre there was a beautiful, painted mandala of the OHM symbol surrounded by flowers.

There were many of us there – both men and women. Shankara, who was running the Sacred Dance Workshop, had chosen some excellent music to resonate with each and all of the chakras. While we watched the sun go down and the full moon come up she led us in dance in a circle. It was a magical evening.

THE SEED OF AN IDEA

In September that year I wrote in my diary: *'I had a feeling to create a food forest, where there will be an abundance of food for the future. I am reading everything about it by Geoff Lawton.'*

Geoff Lawton was one of the first people to promote this form of permaculture, where the planting is fully integrated to provide everything that is needed for self-sustainability of both man and forest. He has taught people all over the world how to make a food forest, even in desert conditions where people have little food.

A food forest consists of seven layers made up of a variety of trees, shrubs, and herbaceous plants

, ground cover and climbing plants, all serving their particular purposes. Some trees are fast growing so that you can chop off branches and drop them to the ground to help build up the soil fertility. Fungus from the rotting wood runs round the forest floor also feeding the plants and trees. Certain plants, trees, and shrubs are grown to fix nitrogen in the soil. Companion plants are used next to trees and other plants to help attract beneficial insects and to keep disease away. Medicinal plants and herbs are also incorporated into the planting. Done correctly, the forest should take care of itself after seven years.

HORTICULTURAL LESSONS FROM YANNIS

I met Yannis from Greece at Ciel Azul and invited him to visit me.

'Yannis has a great knowledge from a young boy of working with the earth. He is so interested in all aspects of nature and talks to plants as I do - just the person I need to teach me where to plant things in a food forest.'

When he came to the house he told me that it was not a good place to be doing what I wanted to do because dust from the road running alongside the field was spreading over everything.

Another interesting thing that he told me was that nurseries cut the taproot of trees so that they can plant them in pots, but it is the taproot that reaches in to the ground to find water. So it takes a long time for it to grow again when it is planted out.

I had been told that fruit trees needed lots of water in summer. Apparently this is not right. Yannis told me that trees and plants tell you when they need water. I had been overwatering them and that had made the leaves dry up.

Another diary entry from around this time reads: *'I have already found that there are many fruit trees that I did not know existed. I feel I am doing what my soul wants me to do, as people are being sent to help me.'*

Before too long I would be learning a lot more about fruit trees that I hadn't know anything about.

chapter fourteen

Clouds on the Horizon

'Since working organically I have noticed that butterflies are coming in to the garden. Today there was a brown speckled butterfly with blue on its wings, exciting to see them.'

I had wanted to live in that house for life, but apparently it was not to be. I started to have problems with my landlord. To begin with he kept coming into my garden any time, just treating it as if he lived there, so that I felt I had no privacy.

Then he refused to allow me to put in a log burner. The fireplace, as it was, just belched smoke out into the room, and sent all the heat up the chimney, so it did little to provide warmth in the room. I was so cold without a log fire. Even with both electric and gas fires on all day it was still not warm.

Martin came round one day. Noticing how cold the place was he managed, ingeniously, to install a log fire for me by blocking off the bottom of the chimney with some wood that had a hole in it to take a flue that could go up the chimney. It was the kind of stove that the Spanish used to use and could easily be removed. It was very efficient so, thanks to him, I was nice and warm in the end.

Something else that the landlord didn't seem to understand was permaculture and green living. Or else he didn't want to know. He didn't like the eco toilet that I had put in, or my rainwater collecting butts.

I had been thinking about putting solar panels on the roof. Then I met Robert who installed them and had been doing so for several years. He agreed to come over to explain everything to me.

I was amazed at how the right people always came along at the right time.

He came over in October to explain what would be involved. His partner, Patricia, acted as interpreter for my landlord, but in the end he refused to give permission for the installation. He did not want holes in the wall, he said, nor batteries on the floor.

Almost as a last straw Vincent, who had been going to

come again and help me for the winter, sent word at the eleventh hour to say that he couldn't come. I was beginning to think that these were all signs suggesting a move elsewhere. Then, funnily enough, a few days later I saw another car with four nines – that number that signifies endings and completion.

My diary log for that time spelled out my feelings quite clearly: *'I really thought I was meant to be here for life. I told them I wanted to do organic gardening and they sprayed the olive trees with poison that was drifting onto where the vegetables were to be grown.'*

'When Thomas, the man lodging with me at the time, asked him: "Please do not spray the trees," the owner simply replied, "I have been doing it for thirty years." When Thomas said, "It will make you ill," the man's answer was simply, "I will go into hospital and take pills." Shows how conditioned he is.

I am so upset at how Mother Earth is being bombarded from the land and skies with pollution, not to mention cars and industry. I am trying desperately to do my little part in healing the earth.

So there needs to be another new start, quite a challenge. I am at present potting up plants that I put in for bees and butterflies and other insects. It's amazing how many bees have already come. I have just been told that if you rent a house they are entitled to keep all the plants you put in, surely this cannot be right! What is the world coming to!

So now I am looking for land where I can create my food forest.'

chapter fifteen

Interesting People

BRIAN

One Sunday, when I was visiting Casita Verde, I met Brian who was cooking their superb Sunday meals. He told me about his life. It's interesting how the son of a moneyed family, a very well-spoken, public-school-educated man, chooses a simple life as a volunteer at Casita Verde, living in a cave. He said he and his brother were like chalk and cheese. I could have listened to him all day. He was the brother who had the courage to live his life as he wanted, not as society would have programmed him. Good for him.

PHILIP

Philip gave me a sound healing massage, using a huge gong, and singing bowls to support his massages with sound.

He placed the singing bowls on the parts of my body that needed healing so that the sound would reverberate through the body. To end he used the largest gong. The sound reverberated through my body in waves. It was very relaxing. During the session I had with him I had a very clear image of a young owl looking out of a nest. I think that the owl is my bird.

Philip is another well-educated young man who has travelled the world extensively, visiting many countries and living life on the edge at times. Once, while he was in Brazil he had felt intuitively that he should leave the place where he was. But he did not heed his intuition and ended up being robbed with a gun in his mouth - how frightening!

He also had some wonderful experiences, though. On another occasion, when he was walking through the jungle during one of his trips, he came to a lake. There, tied up on the shore, was a boat. Wanting to connect with nature, he took the boat out to the middle of the lake and lay down in it. When he looked up to the sky above him he saw a perfect formation of brightly coloured parrots. It was an experience, he said, that he would never forget.

Philip was also making very upmarket Yurts. He lived in

one while he was in Ibiza, before he returned to England to be close to his ailing mother.

chapter sixteen

Like-Minds, New Friends

My Spanish teacher told me about Marcus, who was doing permaculture near Ibiza town. I rang and invited him to come for coffee, to see what I was doing on the plot in Balafia.

It turned out that Marcus' job was to assess how petrol fumes from planes and hire cars affect the environment. With so many visitors to the island every year, this was a serious concern. By measuring the emissions he could assess the impact on the environment and then advise property owners how much tree planting would be needed to combat the pollution. Apparently, the government was behind the scheme. I was pleased to know that something like this was happening.

He invited me to go to see his permaculture land and I went the following week. He had many young people working there for him, running an organic vegetable stall, installing eco-toilets and creating a fruit forest on his huge piece of land with very good soil. It was an interesting day out and I did learn a lot from that visit.

I learnt about APAEEF, the Association of Organic Agricultural Producers on Ibiza and Formentera. It was an organisation that had been established in 2001 for the purpose of promoting organic farming on the islands. I also heard about Ecofeixes, a co-operative of organic growers, that APAEEF was supporting by creating a land bank.

Marcus told me about a woman called Sonia who was co-ordinating the land releases that I had read about in an article in *Del Todo* Newspaper. It was a report that farmers were releasing land for permaculture. I had thought that the land releases would only be for farmers, but Marcos suggested I get in touch with Sonia anyway.

GOOD FRIENDS

With all the setbacks to my plans for the house and garden I was becoming quite disheartened. It was proving difficult to find the land where I could fulfil my dream of creating a fruit forest, so it was a welcome distraction to have a good friend from the USA come to stay with me for a few days in October.

'My friend Bruce, whom I met in Goa is coming to stay with me for twelve days. He is coming from San Francisco. I have lost interest in the garden and am going to enjoy my time with Bruce. He was going to come two years ago and then, at the last minute, he'd had to do jury service.'

I was grateful that he was able to come this time. We explored the island together. We went to new beaches that I had not visited before – there are beautiful beaches and stunning views all round this magical island.

Towards the end of his stay we went to mantra singing at Solara's retreat and really enjoyed the evening. The day after the mantra singing my friend Sheila joined us on an expedition to Es Vedra.

I had first met Sheila on one of Toby's walks - she's his mother – and I had felt an immediate affinity with her. That connection was reinforced when we discovered that we shared a passion for plants. Then, like wayward school children during the walks, we would keep lagging behind everyone else to stop and look at the flowers and plants.

At Es Vedra with Bruce that day we had a picnic in the cave that overlooks the island. The sea was calm and the view of one or two boats sailing in front of the island was so peaceful. Afterwards we went down to Cala Comte beach to watch the sunset. We were blessed with the sunshine all day. On the other side of the island there was cloud all day.

At the end of the day we drove in to Ibiza town to buy costumes for Halloween the following night. The Chinese shop was full of people buying costumes. Halloween is a big thing on Ibiza, but then it's a place where people seem to find any excuse to have a party! Halloween night was a super way to enjoy Bruce's last night of his stay with me after an action-packed week.

COMMON INTERESTS

One day I went to buy a fire lighter at a ferreteria (a hardware shop). I asked the lady next to me if she spoke English and would she be able to ask for one for me in Spanish. She could see some at the end of the shop and took me over to show me as she also wanted one and kept forgetting to buy it.

After we had paid and had left the shop, she asked me my name. When I said, "Siriya" She replied, "I have been wanting to meet you." Christo at Casita Verde had told her about me, that I lived near her and that I was interested in permaculture. That's why she had been looking for me. She had written to me on Facebook and I had not answered - I probably hadn't seen her message. Carolina was her name and she had already asked two other ladies if they were Siriya. Now the universe had brought us together – MAGIC! We decided to start a gardening group for other like-minded people to get together to exchange plants and organic seeds.

One of the people who joined us was Sylvie. When she had arrived in Ibiza she had brought eighty plants with her from Italy. As they increased in size she readily shared them with friends.

Hélène was someone else we met. Her daughter, Natacha, was working with permaculture in Mallorca. Once, when she came to visit us all she brought some organic seeds for me. I was especially pleased with organic sweet corn, as it was so difficult to come by. Before too long knowing Natacha was to prove to be a real bonus for me in so many ways.

It was greatly inspiring to find kindred spirits. I wrote: *'So grateful to have these lovely people to share with and to be able to talk gardening with.'*

SOLARA

A friend of mine, Mia, had told me about Solara's meditations and channellings long before I eventually met her. It wasn't until the end of 2014, when I finally started to go to meditations at her house, Casa Solara, that I met her.

Solara An Ra is a spiritual teacher who runs retreats all around the world, guiding people to heightened enlightenment through meditation and channelled messages. As an 11.11 person – someone who understands the angels' messages – she is doing great work for the community. Many young people, many of them healers themselves, are guided to her for inspired direction. She has a beautiful retreat centre, Casa Solara, just outside Santa Eulalia, where she hosts regular meditations and monthly mantra singing.

There is also a community garden at her house, where people can come and work in exchange for payment in kind - some of the organic vegetables that are grown there.

Once a month she holds community lunches, when people meet to exchange news and information, and share dishes of food that everyone brings along. It is great way of bringing together the many young people who are constantly arriving on the island to start a new life. Many come with young families. It's an excellent network hub for people to promote their activities on the island.

In December that year, 2014, I took seven people to the Community Lunch there. After the lunch we formed a circle and everyone talked about what they were doing. It was a very enjoyable day.

It was good to learn that there would also be a Christmas community lunch for people spending the festive season on their own then. What a wonderful idea! You need never be lonely on Ibiza.

OPENING TO CHANNELLING

Also that December Solara held a three-day retreat for people to channel our higher selves and our spirit guides. We were eight: Ernesto, Dolores, Veetmaya, Katie and Annalisa (from Brighton), Solara and myself.

Solara had been concerned that I had planned to go on a day-retreat on the Monday of the channelling retreat, and would miss one day of hers. In the end the day-retreat was cancelled. I believe the Universe changed it because I was meant to be doing the channelling.

We started at 10 in the morning. First we did breathing exercises to get in touch with our bodies, and followed that with some meditation before trying out our channelling skills. On the first day nothing came to me when I tried to channel, but it happened for me on the second day. That was such a surprise.

chapter seventeen

The Continuing Saga of My Search for Land

My quest to find the land for my fruit forest continued. In December I wrote:

'I went to look at a house near San Carlos today. It was in a perfect location for me - surrounded by pine-covered mountains. There were many trees on the land: almonds, figs, and an apricot tree. I would have been able to make a food forest. I thought this was the place until I saw the house. I have never seen such a hotchpotch of parts built onto one another. The kitchen was so small, with only an old gas fridge and nothing much else to speak of in it, and it was all very old.'

'We went out of the kitchen into a large lounge that was being painted. There was one piece of furniture in it. You then had to go outside again to get to a room at

the end. It would have been very cold in winter.
Upstairs they had built another room where there were
magnificent views. There was no electricity. Water had
to be brought in. It would have cost €10,000 to install
solar energy. The landlady asked how me much I would
offer in rent. I said €800 a month, thinking really that
was too much, but incredibly the woman walked away
in disgust, saying she wanted €1500 a month. These
people are getting very greedy, I don't like it.'

Later I found another house to rent near San Carlos. It
had everything that I wanted - three bedrooms, one
with an en suite and a bath, double-glazing, a lounge,
and a separate kitchen - all brand new. There was
about an acre of land. I explained to the owners what I
wanted to do to create a fruit forest. I tried to explain
how ploughing the land disturbs the insects and
enzymes in the soil and causes it to dry out more
quickly, and I asked them not to plough. I offered to
pay a deposit but they refused, saying it was too big for
me, and too expensive. Basically, they didn't want me
there. I don't think they understood what a food forest
was. The farmers are paid to plough the land every
year, which disturbs everything that's within the soil
and causes it to dry up.

Finding somewhere to manifest my vision of creating a
fruit forest by looking for a rented property on the

ordinary rental market was proving to be a hopeless quest.

Rents were going up year on year, which was making it ever more difficult for me to fulfil my dream, so I decided to try and get some of the land that Marcus had told me was being released for permaculture. That way, at least I would be able to plant my food forest.

I needed to get in touch with Sonia, whom Marcus had said was co-ordinating land releases for permaculture. After many unanswered phone calls and text messages, I did eventually manage to make contact with her and we arranged to meet in San Raphael. She told me she had found some land belonging to a man that was more open than some Ibizencos, and was interested in what I wanted to do. But he was in Barcelona at the time. I would have to wait until he came to the island to talk things through. So now I had to really trust.

chapter eighteen

Past Lives

Sylvie, Carolina and I went for lunch at Casita Verde. I met a healer called Gilles who told me, then and there, that he could see spirits around me.

The following day I went on a walk with Saskia, whom I had met at the Breath Week. We walked from the mountain where she lives to San Vincente, retracing steps that people have trodden over the centuries before cars or roads. While we were walking she told me that she had had a session with a man called Gilles, who had told her about her past life from a reading from a snippet of her hair.

I was intrigued to be hearing about the same man on two consecutive days. It seemed like a sign, so as soon as I reached home I rang him to make an appointment.

I arranged to go the following morning.

Gilles is a Radionics practitioner. Radionics is a diagnostic and healing system that works by reading and adjusting the energy frequencies that are moving through a person's body, using a "witness" from that person (such as a piece of hair) that is placed in the Radionics Box.

After cutting a small piece of my hair to use as a "witness" and placing it in the Box, he started my reading and slowly cleared my many blocks and my Karma.

He told me that I had deep damage to my aura, that my deceased husband was still present, and that both my father and grandfather were weighing me down. He also told me that somebody had put a curse on me thirty-six years earlier.

He said that I had been with my husband during forty lifetimes over a period of 86,000 years. I had also spent forty previous lives with my boyfriend Danny who, he told me, is my energetic partner.

Danny is someone I met many years ago. We had a relationship then and I was still thinking about him ten years later, wondering how he was. Now I understood why I had such a strong connection to him.

Gilles told me that I had been with my eldest daughter for thirty-two earlier lifetimes and with my younger daughter for twenty-one lifetimes. I had spent thirty-two lifetimes with my mother and one lifetime as an aborigine, 12,000 years ago. Very interesting! He told me that my energetic level was 86.02, the highest that I could be.

Later on I recorded that, *'Since my treatment with Gilles it is as if I have had a lot of baggage lifted from me. I feel so light and happy and full of love. I have been working hard to clear everything internal from the past few years - think I must be nearly there. Whether I am right or not, I don't know, but I believe people are sent to me for a purpose - Gilles being one of them.'*

The huge variety of amazing healers on the island was astounding

chapter nineteen

Facing The Unknown – Having to Trust

February 2015: *'I wanted to go out for a pre-birthday meal tomorrow. In the morning I asked the universe for company. After channelling with Solara, she said she would come with me. I am so lucky. We had a great meal together on the beach in the sunshine listening to the waves.'*

The Universe was reminding me to trust. I needed to trust more than ever now as the time approached to leave the house in Balafia. Time was running short before I had to move out.

Then, unexpectedly, just a few days before I was due to go on 3rd March I was told I could stay for another three weeks.

'I feel that the Universe has allowed me this to give me

a little more time.'

It was much-needed extra time that I used well, still searching for 'my land'.

Sylvie and Mario told me about some Italian friends who would let me make a food forest and grow organic vegetables that I could supply their restaurant with. But my heart sank when we went to meet them and I saw where it was. To begin with, the soil was not red and I felt I needed to work on red soil. In Mayan astrology I am Red Earth. Besides, the water had to be brought in by tanker. It could have been the perfect place, as they wanted to do retreats and I could teach people about permaculture, but somehow my intuition told me it was not right.

Then I followed up on another lead that I had now been told of - some land that had already been used for permaculture. Apparently it had water, a greenhouse, and a casita so I thought that, at the last minute, this would be the place. When I arrived there I found a steep hill down to the valley and such a bad access road that would be difficult to get a car down.

Apart from that, the location was perfect but the land had not been used for three years and was full of brambles. The greenhouse had been ripped up by the wind and there was only half of it left. And there was no water. The casita was just a stone room with a single bed, an outside kitchen, and no bathroom.

Astonishingly, the owner kept saying that she wanted to let it to holiday makers and I wondered if people would know what they would be coming to! She also told me that I could not have people working for me, as she had had hippies in the past and had had problems with them. So it was a no-go from the start and another big disappointment.

MOVING OUT

'Now I have nine days to find somewhere to live. This needs a great deal of trust. I have no roof over my head and all my compost, mulching, eco toilet, guttering, compost maker, and the things from the house need to be stored somewhere.

A friend said he would put my compost in his field and then, at the last minute told me he couldn't. Another young man agreed that he would help me move and then he too said he couldn't.'

I was feeling down and let down but then once again the Universe sent me help in the form of good, loyal friends.

'Mario and Sylvie are my saviours. They will look after my stuff in their garage and put some compost and the

guttering and some other bits and pieces in their field. They have 100 fruit trees and plants of mine.'

Dear Cathy, saying that I needed to get a place to stay, went to Santa Eulalia to book a hostel for me. I went to meditation with Solara and she said she would put some of my compost on her land.

Amazingly all kinds of helpful people turned up at the last minute to help me.

Carolina told me about a man who did removals; Elizabeth agreed to take my cold frame and some plants to look after for me.

Then I went to a healing afternoon, where people were doing crystal healing, massage, and reflexology and met Sarah. She told me that she had heard about me at City Airport in London and had wanted to meet me ever since! She was the one who then found me a place to put all the rest of my stuff in a field at Abraham's.

Abraham was a beautiful soul who looked after abandoned animals. At that time he had two horses, and goats, pigs, ducks, and twenty-five dogs. His only work was as a waiter, so it must have been difficult for him. The animals there all looked very happy, especially the dogs. They were playing with each other in the field.

The day for moving dawned. Martin was the only friend who had made me promises of help and didn't let me down. He had moved back to Ibiza just the day before I had to move and he had no car. His had broken down and he could not afford to have it mended. In spite of that, though, he was true to his word and gallantly turned up to help on an old motorbike.

In the end everything went smoothly. Solara and Ernesto helped me move some compost and mulching to their field. Sylvie and Mario came to take the guttering, the eco toilet, the compost maker, the piping, and all sorts of other bits and pieces. Martin helped pack the van with Mario. In the afternoon Chris Pearson came to move all the rest of the stuff. He and Martin worked well packing the van together.

Chris told me that he had started working when he was just fourteen. He was now thirty-one years old, had a gas specialist company in England, and was living in Ibiza with his wife and two children. They had come to find a better way of life in a place where life was so great for children. I really admired that young man.

Afterwards, at the end of the day, I wrote, *'The day of 24th March 2015 has dawned; last minute things had to be moved. Cathy helped me pack the car and get everything into the hostel in Santa Eulalia. So now I am settled, making the room homely. Along with lettuce, parsley, and spinach plants to make salads, flowers adorn the balcony to brighten up the day. It is raining today. I can now chill out for a while.*

When I left the house I decided to surrender everything, and go into the flow, and live in the moment and see what happens.

My friend Sheila has taken over my house. She will keep the garden organic. She was worried that she would not get the house, but I had a feeling that she would and told her so. I felt it was meant for her. She says she is happier there than she has ever been in her life. She also told me people remark on the energies in the garden, probably from the clearing of the land that I did with a special crystal.'

One night, while I was staying at the hostel, I woke up at 00.30 and could hear some music. There was a fiesta in Santa Eulalia.

I decided that, as I was living in town I needed to make the most of it and see what was happening. People were dancing in the street. A band was moving along the lane known affectionately as Restaurant Street playing drums. Jumping jack fireworks were going off beside them and a parade of people was following behind the musicians. The many happy people, the music, the fireworks, the trees festooned with pretty lights all made for a lovely and festive atmosphere.

As I walked towards the Ayuntamiento building in the centre of town I thought to myself, *'This is what I love about Ibiza – you can always find music and happiness.'*

IN SUSPENSE AND SEARCHING

Through the winter months of 2014-2015 it seemed as though my plans to establish a permaculture food forest were finally gaining impetus.

I got news from Sonia. *'Suddenly I have heard from Sonia about the land, she wants me to send her an email to say exactly what I want to do on the land to send to the owner, who is still in Barcelona.'*

I answered immediately and waited with baited breath for her reply. In my mind's eye I was already establishing myself there!

'I am waiting for the owner of the plot that Sonia was telling me about to come back from Barcelona. Then I need to have a wooden house to put on the land. So I need to trust that the owner will let me live there. The government powers that be don't like you putting a

house on the land. It has to be movable, so a wooden house should fit the bill perfectly.

This is just what I have dreamed of and gives me a lot of food for thought. I have to be really trusting that, when the owner of the land comes back from Barcelona, he will agree to let me rent the land and put a wooden house on it.'

I began researching. *'Yesterday I went to Casita Verde to find out about wireless internet. I was talking to Chris about a wooden house, when he told me about Dorus who was going to build wooden wagons made from local and recycled materials. They would be completely self sufficient and off-grid with a composting toilet, a rocket stove that would also provide under floor heating, re-cycled water and solar energy.'*

I was excited and full of ideas for my own new life.

'I went to a permaculture meeting in Santa Eulalia. It was all in Spanish but the leader spoke English. He explained to me that the group is creating a food forest in San Carlos and they were arranging the water supply. There are 560 people in the group, trying to change things on the planet. They bring things to the meeting to exchange. They use a new kind of exchange system, trading work or goods with each other rather

than money. They mark up how much people owe, and repay in kind.

It seems to be a big thing in Ibiza, with people wanting to do permaculture and live an alternative lifestyle more in harmony with nature. I met one couple that would like to build houses of mud - adobe houses. They would blend in beautifully with the landscape - far better than the huge houses that blight the island, built by and for the people with money. But there are so many restrictions on living accommodation on the land that make it difficult for ordinary people.'

Another three pieces of land came up. One of them was in a beautiful valley where there were already some fruit trees, but it was down an unused lane that had dropped away steeply in one place. The accommodation consisted of three rooms that had been for the animals. There was just one tiny window in one of the rooms. They had built a kitchen in the end room, but there was no bathroom. They told me I could build one on, but that would have been impossible. There was no room in the kitchen for an access door to it - you would have had to go outside every time. It was a shame because it was a super spot, with miles of woods and valley all around, but it simply was not suitable.

The other two places were just too small.

chapter twenty

Channellings

In April 2015 I had more channellings. *'There have been two channellings with Solara this week. One was from the order of Melchizedek, telling me to use the name Siriya - a name that has a special vibration and is given to me by them to attract my star seeds. Three days later I had a lovely channelling. It was quite overwhelming and brought tears to my eyes. It went on for 5.05 minutes and then the battery switched off.'*

'Siriya, Siriya, Siriya! You are twice-fold initiated into the frequency of your name, this time accompanied by the Melchizedek frequency that is also yours. This new frequency that beams out from you now will bring you into a greater sense of peace and clarity within yourself. It is not that you are not peaceful and clear, it is just that you will have greater periods of clarity and stillness within yourself - total bliss within your experience of yourself and earth life. You are a frequency keeper within your very nature, but you

were not able to hold this frequency surrounded by your family and husband because of the disparity between their frequency and yours. Now that you are separated, you are moving into the frequency that is naturally yours - on a higher dimensional level - and when you are on your land, you will set up a type of crystal grid to assist with the activation of a portal there.' The group holds hands in a Namaste.

Siriya: 'I AM SIRIYA OF THE LIGHT!'

chapter twenty one

Summer in Cala Nova Campsite

As May came to an end my stay at the Hostel during the winter months had also to draw to a close. The accommodation was going to be needed for seasonal summer rents.

I had been there for seven weeks and needed to leave by 26th May.

I had a feeling that I could perhaps stay on the campsite at Cala Nova. I had visited friends staying there in the past and I'd liked the place. Cathy had also suggested that I move there and then, when Sheila sent me a link to someone who was selling a caravan, I took it as a sign as to my next step.

'On Sunday I went to see the caravan. It was quite old and smaller than I thought it would be, and many

things were broken, but I had to have somewhere to live and, as I had to get out of the hostel by 26th May, I didn't have time to look for another one. I decided that, with a bit of ingenuity, I could make the best of the space. I could store some of my stuff under the seats and an awning outside would also give me extra space.

I asked the seller, Willie, if he would put it on the campsite for me, and we arranged to move it there on May 11th. So I will have a few days to sort things out before moving in on the Saturday. Willie also offered to help me find an awning.'

There was also good news from the campsite. I could have plot number 1, which was just inside the gate. That number 1 again! Even better, the campsite owner said I could bring all my plants and trees. It was a big relief to know that I could have my plants around me.

'Great excitement today the 11th May (divine number) - my caravan is being delivered to the campsite.'

When Willie arrived he said he was going to have difficulty getting the caravan through the narrow space with a car. At that moment I happened to turn around and came face to face with a couple behind me who told me that they had the same caravan. They suggested taking it off the tow bar and moving it by hand. Then they helped us to get it into place.

Another synchronicity! Amazing!

Thinking about everything that had been going on recently I wrote: *'I did not think so much would be happening to me at my age of seventy-nine. I imagined myself living a quiet life painting pictures and pottering in a garden. Now a whole new life has evolved for me, and who knows what's next. I am on a divine path and decided to just go with the flow and listen to my heart. I have a few days to get the caravan ready before leaving the Hostel. It is a really hot week, unusual for this time of year. I am so lucky as Willie has put two shelves up for me, given me a mattress and mosquito net.'*

Once I had arrived at the campsite I felt content with the move.

'This is my first day in the caravan on a beautiful site near the beach, under pine trees. At the moment it is quiet here.'

And I began to make the most of being so close to a beach and the sea.

'This morning I arrived at the beach early morning, as usual, to do my meditation and yoga. Every day the sea is in a different mood. Today there are big waves pounding the rocks. Young men are out on their boards

*running along the waves. Yesterday the sea was gently
lapping the shore, the sun reflecting in the water, the
wind gently playing round my shoulders. A nude man
walks along the beach silhouetted against the sun, an
azure sky above.'*

I had some shading erected to keep the caravan a bit
cooler. Solara had been channelled to come and help
me. She came with Ernesto and they took me to
Decathlon, the outdoors specialist shop in Ibiza, to buy
a table and an outside light. When we got back they
put up a fly screen for me. I already had a table to put
the small cooker on and two electric plates to cook on.
Another table that fitted under it was perfect for
cutlery and a few cooking utensils.

The tents and caravans on the campsite were set
under pine trees. There was one man on site who was
constantly raking up the needles. I hadn't realised how
many pine needles fall all the time, and they get into
everything. Before I had put up my tent extension they
had got into my cooker outside and made everything
outside dirty. The canopy extension made things so
much better.

I spent the next two weeks moving all my plants and
trees to the campsite. It was quite exhausting, but
most rewarding. My small patch of campsite soon
started to look like a garden and it felt so much more

like home when I was surrounded by my family of fruit trees, flowering shrubs, herbs and vegetable plants. I had chosen many of them specifically to attract bees and other insects, and even after just one day there, one of the shrubs had bees busily buzzing around it. I was particularly fascinated by one unusual bee-like insect. It hovered over one of my plants just like a humming bird.

One day, when I had just arrived back with a car full of plants, Marcia, a young woman that I know, just happened to be there to do her washing on the campsite. She kindly helped me to move the plants but when she saw my caravan she realised that it was not level. I would never have noticed! The next day she brought her boyfriend Ewen with a spirit level and they levelled it up for me. I felt so lucky.

Ewen was a young Frenchman selling obelisks in the market. He was trying to attract people's attention to a special crystal that clears the atmosphere. By spreading magnetised prismatic rays into the sky it cleans the waters and helps the earth to regenerate itself. Importantly it brings the "water dragons" back to life – and as we now know, water carries consciousness

Ewen explained that this crystal is the remedy that the earth has generated to rebirth itself. It is dressed with five different metals. Among them are radioactive

Cobalt to regulate radiations in the atmosphere, Citrin to open the sky and Clear Quartz, which has a complete range of frequencies

Ewen had climbed posts and trees all over the island to put the obelisk up high in fifty-five places to clear the controversial aircraft chemtrails that we had begun to see so much more often.

GAIA MEDITATION

On May 24th I went to a planetary meditation at Es Vedra. The purpose was to raise the Vibration of Gaia, to help manifest her into 5D Earth. Our intention was to bring change on the earth for all animals, plants, trees, and ourselves and free us from any current restrictions.

I travelled with three others. We parked the car and walked through woods. As we emerged we saw the magical rock island rising majestically out of a calm sea and shrouded in cloud. It always made me feel serene when I was there.

People were gathering in a circle on the flat area on the high cliff that overlooks the island. It is a very peaceful place. More than a hundred and forty souls had come for the meditation, and others, who had really come just to see Es Vedra, joined with us. It was a truly memorable day.

Solara smudged everybody with a special sage from America to clear our auras before the ceremony. Pete and Kinan led the meditation and Elena Texidor led the Kundalini Mantra, accompanied by Trace Harris on his drum. It was an amazing gathering with an awesome vibe. One nation in a groove, all looking for change.

On our way there Solara told us how, the previous day, a sudden and unexpected tornado had whipped up all the loose straw in the field next to her house, then dumped it on her house. She had many guests staying at the time. Later she was channelled that it was to clear the bad energies in the house.

LIFE ON THE CAMPSITE

The morning after the Gaia Meditation I went down to the beach to do some yoga at 7 o'clock before the sun got too hot.

'It's great listening to the waves. Some days the sea is gentle with the sun reflecting off the water, like jewels sparkling in the ocean. On other days huge waves pound the shore. The surfers are out early on those days. Meditating and breathing in the clean salty air is a bonus. I lay down on the sand to relax afterwards and looked up at the clear blue sky. My eye caught

sight of a tuft of yellow daisies perched on the edge of a rock. It always amazes me that plants can grow in such dry, stony soil. It reminded me of the desert in South Africa where I had the good fortune to see a burst of magnificent colour after the rain, when the desert blooms and the fields of colour stretch as far as the eye can see - nature at its best.'

I began to have some insights into why I had been guided to move onto the campsite.

'This week I was channelled to clear the campsite of bad energies, I knew there was a reason for me being here. I have noticed since living on the campsite, that people with nothing, living from day to day, trusting in the universe, are far more happy than those who have a great deal of money and are unable to share it because of fear of having nothing.'

'People with nothing don't have to worry about people taking advantage of them. If you have nothing, nobody can steal from you. I noticed many light workers are living from hand to mouth, but they always have enough food and somewhere to live. I recently read a very inspiring book by a former businessman, Mark Boyle, called "The Moneyless Man." In it he relates why he chose to find a way of challenging monetary economics and how he found ways of living a normal life, relying instead on such things as seasonal foods,

renewable energy, skill-swap groups and more.'

'There is a couple here in the next tent who come from Holland, Bianca and Arno. He was not very positive, so I taught them both to say: "I am happy, I am healthy I am wealthy, I am secure, I am worthy, I am grateful, I am positive, I am beautiful, I am blessed, I am confident, I am courageous, I am excited about today." They wrote it on a piece of paper and pinned it to their tent and looked at it every day. Arno is now more positive. He is making a website to promote security in villas, saying he will be a billionaire. If he keeps positive, I am sure he will. They were looking for a house to rent in the winter. When they found one they liked they were the ones chosen to be the tenants out of twenty others who went to see it.'

In May and June it was very quiet with mainly long-term people staying there.

'There is a huge mix of people. There are many healers - Reiki practitioners, an Osteopath, massage therapists, a Pedicurist There's also a Del Boy wheeler dealer, who is an interesting man and very kind and helpful.'

Later on, once the season had kicked in and things had become busier – *'as July and August arrive tents are crammed in to every nook and cranny'* - I had a different story to tell, a story that told of the darker side of life on the island.

'The campsite is very noisy, day and night. The sound of people playing guitars and drums reverberates round the campsite at all times. I couldn't sleep as, even after the music had stopped, people nearby were still talking. At three in the morning I decided to go to the beach and meditate. I sat in front of a stack of sunbeds by the sea and then, after meditating for a while I suddenly felt a hot wind behind me, as if someone had turned on a fire. And an unusual smell - like the tropical weather in Thailand - very weird. And I could not smell the sea. I have also been itching and feeling slight dizziness recently. I read on Galactic News, that it is all part of the Ascension - nice to have confirmation of what is happening.'

'Many people are completely lost - it is so sad. They have little money and are on drugs, and smoking and drinking to excess. So many of the youngsters here have difficulty getting jobs and, when they do get one, are paid a pittance for working hard for long hours. One friend, Niki, has been working in a hot kitchen cooking breakfasts from 10am to 6pm, and is not given any food or even water for the whole day. Another young man has to hitch a lift to the centre of the island every day - not an easy task - just to wash dishes all day.'

'And there are the dramas being played out. One French woman here has a thirteen-year-old daughter but I did not even know she had a daughter, as she is always on her own, smoking dope and drinking alcohol when I see her. She has even taught her daughter to smoke! Unbelievable! The poor child is not looked after properly and dragged from one place to another, with no fixed abode. The poor girl needs some love and attention. It's no surprise that she set fire to the toilet rolls in a plastic container in the bathrooms. Luckily Niki in the caravan next to me has a strong sense of smell and went to investigate - nobody nearby to the bathrooms seemed to smell it. We could have had the whole place on fire.'

chapter twenty two

Mallorca

Natacha was the young woman that I had met through my gardening friends who shared my passion for plants.

I wanted to go and stay with her for a while, on her permaculture farm in the mountains. She had invited me to go for three or four weeks. I could help her to pick the fruit, she said, then learn how to dry it.

Sitting outside my caravan amongst my plants I suddenly had the thought that, at the present moment, I could be free to go if there were someone to water my plants. I mentioned it to Niki and she offered to water them, saying that she would find it relaxing. Then Natacha told me that she would be coming over to Ibiza to celebrate her father's sixtieth birthday on 8th July and suggested that we could travel back together the following day.

I was very excited at the thought of going and had a strong feeling that this was meant to be.

On 9th July we caught the ferry at Ibiza Port and, after a four-hour crossing arrived at 00.30. Natacha drove us through the night for half an hour passing Inca, the nearest big town to her place, then Selva and on to Caimari, her closest village.

I'd had no expectations when she'd invited me to stay with her, but Natacha is a girl after my own heart living the kind of lifestyle that I admire.

I had a room to myself with a futon on the floor. In the daylight, the morning after we arrived, I looked out at the surrounding countryside with its magnificent mountains. It was just the kind of landscape that I love.

She showed me around the place. She was creating a thoroughly unpolluted living space. The windows of the house were always open to let in the clean air. She had no grid electricity. There was one solar panel and two portable solar lights that she charged in the sun during the day to give enough light for the evening.

She also had no fridge or washing machine. During the summer she would fill a huge bowl with cold water then soaked the clothes for some time, before putting in soap and dancing on the washing. It was surprising how clean she got it. During the winter, though, a friend let her use her washing machine.

Outside she had a compost toilet that she had made herself by placing a bucket between two palm logs. The logs were topped with a tile on each and resting on the tiles, spanning the bucket was a shaped log to sit on. She used wood chips and leaves to cover the waste. At night, to save us having to go outside for a pee there, we used a bucket with some water in it if we needed to go. We would then use it to feed the flowers, but didn't use it on the vegetables.

When she showed me around her garden she explained how she made her compost in layers, using dried grass and leaves, dried plants, donkey manure, and anything else that she could find that would rot down. She had many worms working the compost and it ended up like beautiful soil, just right to feed her plants. She also soaked symphytum (comfrey) in water for three days as a plant feed.

I made a mental note to get some. I had used it as a plant fertiliser in my garden in England and this reminded me that I needed to find some for my plants in Ibiza.

Natacha was so happy with her simple life. There

should be more people like her.

After my first tour of the place we set off at about 11o'clock to go to the market in Inca. To reach it we walked through an area of interesting old buildings. There were many stalls selling fruit, vegetables, plants, and all manner of other things. Wanting to eat produce that had come from the island as much as possible, we first made our way to a stall selling local vegetables and fruit. Then we went to a stall of organic foods. After that we went to two bio shops, before heading back for lunch.

While Natacha prepared the meal I shelled dry peas ready for planting the next year.

After lunch we went to see some land that her father had bought for her to work following permaculture principles. It was set against a backdrop of mountains and there were already many fruit trees there. She had planted more than a hundred - a wide variety of both evergreen and deciduous trees and shrubs. She'd used some to create hedges with plenty of diversity. A friend of hers, Willow, had been helping her and teaching her how to graft trees. She showed me many of the trees that she had already successfully grafted.

Willow, an amazing man in his sixties, was a fund of information about trees - he'd been planting them for over twenty-five years. He was also advising her on what to plant. He had suggested ideas for trees that flower at the same time to make a beautiful display of colour in spring. He'd told her which trees to plant for fixing nitrogen in the soil, such as acacia.

Natacha's vision was to plant plenty of oaks, almonds, figs and olives.

I was getting a lot more ideas as to what to plant on my land, and was glad to know that Willow would be coming to Ibiza the next year to teach me and my friend, Sylvie, about grafting.

One of the problems that Natacha had was that the well dried up in summer, and she had to have water brought to the farm. The tank of water arrived and we watered the fruit trees and vegetables. It was a mammoth job for Natacha on her own, but once the trees would become more established they would not need so much water. And she did have ideas about saving rainwater in the future. We shared a passion for saving water and caring about the environment.

Before we left the plot we picked mint, basil, spinach and tomatoes to take home for our meal and left as the sun was going down after a lovely, eventful day.

'How lucky I am to be staying in this beautiful piece of

heaven-on-earth, with a beautiful soul! I feel so grateful and happy to be here. Who would have thought, when I was in the Hostel in Santa Eulalia, that I would be here in July? Good to go with the flow. I am lucky as, even though I don't have land to grow my own vegetables, I have been guided here, where I can still have organic fruit and vegetables from the garden.'

A WALK IN THE MOUNTAINS

On July 11th we set off early, at 6.40 in the morning, to climb the mountains. It was a perfect day. The skies were blue and there was a cool early morning breeze. Most of the climb was through oak woods, which was a bonus later on as the day warmed up in the heat at that time of year.

We walked along gravel paths and up cobbled steps - there are many on Mallorca - and climbed through the valley flanked by mountains on our left. There were a few other people out early, like us, and some with strong constitutions passed us running or on bicycles.

The scenery changed constantly. As we climbed higher we had spectacular views down the valley in every direction. We walked without talking, with only the sounds of birds, cicadas and goat bells to break the silence. The tang of herbs and trees scented the air as we wound round the many bends until we reached the summit where we stopped to eat something. A magnificent scene of the Sierra de Tramuntana mountain range and distant valleys stretched far away in front of us.

Descending the other side of the mountain, we walked through a beautiful wood of holm oak and, after four hours on our feet, we reached a water tank filled with fresh mountain water. Across the wooded valley the mighty mountain, Puig de Massenella, rose up majestically.

Natacha jumped into the water to cool down while I dangled my legs in the pool and listened to the gentle trickle of water going into the pool. We rested there, under the holm oak wood, in the heat of the day, enjoying our picnic of tomatoes, garlic and onions from the garden, all covered in olive oil and home-made bread - Natacha's home-baked bread. We ate her own dried figs from her garden for afters.

After a rest we walked to the Monastery at Lluc, the island's most important pilgrimage site. It was founded in the 13th century and is also known for its internationally acclaimed boys' choir, Els Blauets. These days the monks' former cells are rented out to visitors. Natacha told me that she had stayed there with her Mum and Dad once and that she had been unable to sleep because she could feel a presence there. Spookily, the locked door to her room had kept on opening!

After we had looked around for a while, and seen where the horses had been tethered underneath the visitor's bedrooms, I felt that I had walked enough for one day and decided to go back by bus. Natacha decided to walk and arrived back three hours later. She had met someone she knew in the village and had stayed to have a drink.

A SIMPLE ECO LIFE

One Sunday morning we left the house at 9 o'clock, taking along a ladder to go the field where Natacha had planted trees. Four years previously she had learnt how to graft fruit onto almond trees and we found the plum graft laden with juicy black plums. She picked a basketful of them that day, enough for a week. I was interested to learn that they can also be grafted onto olive trees.

She had shown the farmer that he had no need to spray with insecticides by pointing out to him that there was more disease on the trees that he had sprayed than on her unsprayed trees. The art of picking fruit, she explained, is to catch it just before it is ripe. It is once it has ripened that the insects get in.

The basket she filled with plums was one that she had made herself. Basket making was another of the skills that she was perfecting. She was making baskets for herself and to sell and was creating beautiful, colourful baskets using all types of canes from many different plants. To date she had used myrtle (myrto), cana, olive and Mediterranean buckthorn (Rhamnus Alaternus), and was trying different ways of enhancing them.

She told me how she had planted many fruit trees and Mediterranean herbs on a plot that was owned by the parents of a boyfriend that she had been seeing for a while. She'd had to leave it when they'd split up. After she'd gone he didn't water the trees and plants, so gradually they were dying. He did not appreciate all the time, effort and passion that she had put into the planting. People do not seem to realise the work that has to be put in to growing trees, how they do need to be watered and looked after. If you plant trees, you need to water them regularly at least twice a week in dry seasons.

It was such a shame.

One day we visited another market, at Santa Maria del Cami, which is a lovely old village with narrow streets nestling under the wings of its impressive church. We arrived at a walkway clothed each side with different varieties of trees. It led to a large tree-lined square where all the organic farmers gathered with their produce.

Natacha led me to the stall of one of her friends who grows everything himself. He specialised in flours, and had a huge range on offer – Kamut (made from an ancient form of wheat called Khorasan), Spelt (another ancient form of wheat that was becoming a very popular alternative to modern wheat), chickpea flour, cornflour, and Xeixa.

Xeixa is another ancient wheat variety that is close to extinction and currently grown only on Mallorca. In the Balearic Islands it has a legendary status, featuring in many stories and poems. As a food it is valuable partly because it is considered to be a more easily digested form of wheat. More importantly, it can be grown on all kinds of terrain and is particularly well suited as a flour for bread that acquires a uniquely aromatic flavour when it is used.

We also stopped to chat to another stallholder, a lady who had lost her husband and was carrying on the work alone. She was offering different types of goat's cheese and also selling fruit and vegetables that she had grown herself. It's intensive work growing fruit and vegetables organically. I did admire her.

We arrived home in time for lunch. Afterwards, as I rested I noted, *'Now I am writing in the shade of an ash tree, with a cool wind blowing round me, looking at puffy white clouds bubbling up behind the mountains, on a hot, hot day. Many birds frequent the garden. I watch a flycatcher sitting on the branch of a dead tree. It's easy to know this bird as it flies off to catch a fly and then comes back to the same branch.*

At 5 this evening we will visit Natacha's farm to water the trees and plants. She will be pleased when her house has been renovated and she can live on her own land. It's not easy - especially in summer - keeping two places with the amount of watering needed. It can take up to two or three hours if she has to do it without help.'

Early one Monday morning we joined a yoga class in a village half an hour away. The teacher was English, of Spanish parents, and she was an excellent teacher, so I signed up to go twice a week until the end of the month. After yoga I relaxed in the shade of my favourite ash tree to read Hilary Carter's book, *Number Woman*.

In the heat of the summer we were active in the early, cool part of the day and then later on, towards the end of the day. The rest of the day was slower and less industrious. I must have been lying under the ash tree when I wrote, *'Today is very hot again, but there is a cooling breeze from the mountains. I listen to the cicadas. Then the frogs start up a chorus that sounds like a saw going through wood. Bird calls follow and bees hum. Then there is silence. The heat is oppressive so no work can be done until later, after 6pm.'*

'Every night, before going to bed, Natacha lies in her hammock, and watches shooting stars. One night she saw a barn owl fly overhead. Many bird calls can be heard at night - the owl and an unusual bird I had not heard before. The cuckoo calls during the day.'

LEARNING ABOUT FRUITS

'Natacha has cooked me the most delicious meals every day, using the produce in her garden. She loves to cook healthy meals for us. I am so lucky. I have always said I would like someone to cook for me. Perhaps they have sent me my angel.'

One morning, in the middle of July, it was a cloudy day and cooler, so we took the opportunity to go picking blackberries. We collected three boxes full and Natacha turned them into blackberry and pear jam.

Another time that we collected blackberries she made blackberry vinegar. She put the blackberries into a stone jar with vinegar and pressed down hard with a perforated implement to squeeze out the fruit juice. She repeated this on alternate days for a week and then it was ready for bottling.

We went to visit a beautiful garden that Willow had planted 25 years previously. There was a magnificent bamboo forest. Bamboo needs damp soil to grow successfully and it was magical to walk through the tall, straight, perfectly vertical stems on that hot summer day.

He had also planted many other trees, including fruit trees. There were several that I had never heard of before. New to me was the one that originates from South Africa, called Dovyalis Caffra, also known as the Kei apple. It has small yellow fruit full of goodness with an unusual taste and it can be eaten fresh or preserved as jam or pickle.

He also had Feijoa, otherwise called Guavasteen or Guava Pineapple, which comes from South America but grows well in cold climates. And, of course, there were the more usual fruit trees - plums, pears, peaches, apples, pomegranate as well as hazelnut and walnut. Everything was laden with fruit.

Learning about these new, exotic fruits reminded me of one of Solara's channelled messages: "There are strands that are being woven. Many, many strands come together to make a basket which is filled with fruit, fruit that you have never heard of."

I remembered the message as I wrote, *'Already I am being brought into contact with unusual fruit trees - Guava Strawberry is a fruit I had never heard of, Fejoia, Dovyalis and a fruit bush I have seen in a nursery. Just a few I have come across since the channelling.'*

We collected apples and pears that had just been left on the trees in the garden that Willow had planted twenty-five years previously that nobody had bothered to harvest. We were going to slice them ready for drying for the winter then Natacha would bag them up and sell them at the market. I wanted to learn how to dry fruit, so this was the perfect opportunity.

During the day, when the sun was hot, Natacha laid the sliced fruit to dry on slatted trays that she had made. When the fruit was nearly dry she would lay it out on fabric during the day, so that it was easier to fold up and bring in under the terrace at night. Once it was really dry, after about five days, she would put it into jars. She showed me how to make the drying slats so that I would be able to make some when I had my food forest up and running.

'We are now in the middle of August. We have cut up apples, kilos of pears, plums, peaches, and now it is fig

time. *There is a solar oven in the garden where she can dry them if the weather is not perfect. I am learning when they are ready to pick. I did not know that there are many varieties of fig - I thought a fig was a fig – and I was excited to find a black fig and also a purple one. The black fig is early and is easy to dry. It turns out that early varieties are best for drying. If they get wet with rain in September they are no good.'*

I also learnt, finally, how to dry tomatoes. *'We now have dried tomatoes, I tried last year and they all went bad. The secret is to use small tomatoes that are not too juicy. Sprinkle with salt, dry face up for two days and then turn over for three days. Put in jars with olive oil. Easy when you know how! Another useful tip, special grass raffia can be use for tying up plants - so much better than string.'*

SYNCHRONICITIES

'Synchronicities are happening all the time. Natacha and I went to an excellent vegetarian, organic restaurant in Inca. They serve four dishes for €11. The menu is different every time. We had just sat down at the table when a Venezuelan friend of Natacha's came in. In the eleven years he had lived on the island he had never been in the restaurant before. He is learning permaculture and his dream is to grow all his own food for his family. He is trying to learn all he can about the

make up of the soil.'

'Natacha suggested that he join us at the beach after the meal, where we were going to meet Willow. He already knew him, so he was pleased to join us. When we arrived at the beach Willow introduced me to Ben who came from Plymouth in Devon, near where I used to live before.'

'Ben came to Mallorca eleven years ago. He used to work with his father, building boats. His father had asked him if he wanted to carry on the business and he had refused, saying that he wanted to opt out. He had met his wife in Mallorca and, since being here he has learnt how to build dry stonewalls and he is keen on permaculture and planting trees. He told me his father was grateful he left the business as it forced him to sell. Now he is enjoying life with no stress. He comes often to Mallorca to stay with his son and his wife.'

CAN LLUC

At the end of July, I took a bus up into the mountains from Caimari to Lluc Monastery to stay overnight at the hostel. I left the house at 8 in the morning to catch the 8.30 bus, only to find that I had been given the wrong information. On Saturdays the bus didn't leave until 10.50. What to do? I did not want to walk back to the house with all my luggage, so I decided to ask the

Universe for a lift. I had never done this before but I managed to hitch a lift with the third car that came along. The driver was a lady who worked at the museum at the Monastery and was happy to take me all the way. That was such good fortune! I arrived at around 11 o'clock.

Lluc has been a holy place of pilgrimage that dates back as far back as Roman times, when it was known as a *lucrus*, meaning sacred forest. Some people believe that that the sanctuary's name is derived from that Latin word but there is one legend that has far more romantic origins.

According to this story, the site had been the hill top farm owned by a Moorish family that had converted to Christianity in order to retain their property from being seized by the Knights Templar. One afternoon, sometime during the 13th century, young Lluc, son of the family, had been tending his sheep and goats at that place when he came across a statue of a black Madonna - some say in the undergrowth; some say in a river. He took it to the local priest at the Church of Sant Pere in Escorca, where it was given pride of place. The next day, however, when people came to worship, the statue had gone again, only to be re-discovered by young Lluc in its original hiding place. Once again, the boy took it to the priest, and once again it returned itself to its first spot.

This sequence of events played out several times before they decided to concede that the statue wanted to stay where it was found. So they decided to build a chapel on the site where it had originally been found. That Augustinian hermitage was started in 1260 and subsequently it had been granted ever more important status by various popes to finally become an important pilgrimage destination and home of the Es Blauets Boys' Choir.

These days it is a major stopping point for many visitors to the island. Some come as pilgrims to pray and worship at the Gothic Black Madonna; some come on retreat to this place that is considered to be Mallorca's spiritual home. Most come for just a few hours to admire the magnificent Basilica, visit the museum and explore the grounds and Botanical Gardens. And, because of its perfect setting in the mountains, it is also a favourite starting point for hikers.

I had not pre-booked but was lucky enough to get a room at the hostel. They gave me an electronic card for room number 221. Synchronicity was at work again - this was the same number as the GR221 walk that I was planning to take. From my room I had a wonderful view overlooking holm oak woods across to the mountains of Serra De Tramuntana. There were clouds drifting over the peaks and a cool breeze was blowing. It was ideal for walking.

A wide paved path with steps led up the mountain from the monastery to a cross at the top. Looking out at the view from the summit, I saw a flat circular valley below, lush with orange and olive trees and other food produce. The surrounding mountains would be covered with snow in winter, so I was surprised to see those orange and olive trees thriving. I decided that it must be very sheltered from the bad weather in winter.

I stopped to sit and meditated there at the top, overlooking that magnificent landscape.

Another wide path led down the other side of the mountain along the Way of the Rosary, past five fine stone monuments with bronze reliefs - works of art created by some well known Spanish architects and artists.

Higher up the mountain is the Font Cuberta - the covered fountain, overseen by a statue of Our Lady of Lluc. It has been providing water for the sanctuary and the hostel since time immemorial. The water is cold and deliciously refreshing after a long walk and many people go to collect it in large bottles.

I walked down a lane and came to a gate where a man, sitting at the entrance, told me that I could not enter, but that I was allowed to walk there on a Sunday. So early the next day, a Sunday, I walked down the road through the holm oak woods, winding around the bends that led to the bottom of the mountain. I came to a valley that I had been able to see from the cross on the mountain and had wanted to explore. There were fincas nestling down there and it turned out that the reason the road was closed during the week was because visitors just threw their rubbish everywhere without a thought of what it does to the environment and the people who live there were tired of clearing up after everyone.

It's so sad that some people desecrate such a lovely place and spoil it for the good of the wildlife and for people's enjoyment. Whenever I am out walking I find myself picking up plastic bottles, cerveza tins and coca cola cans, not to mention the glass bottles that could start a fire. All thoughtlessly just tossed into the hedges, fields, and orchards. Why can't children at school be taught to care for the environment?

I walked through ancient olive groves and orange trees and I came to a large house, home to an agricultural school for youngsters. Beyond that I carried on, meandering along the valley, always wanting to see what is around the next corner. I climbed over a mountain and into another valley surrounded by mountains. There, in the heart of the mountains, I sat down to enjoy the beautiful surroundings. By now I had been walking for an hour and the sun was beginning to beat down on me, so I decided to get back before it got too hot. By now, I was quite drained of energy so it did take me quite long time to climb back up the mountain road.

The following day I took the bus back to Caimari.

A VISIT TO A YURT

One day we were invited to a baby's birthday party by a couple that live in a yurt. I was surprised by how much room there is in a yurt, and by how much light comes in through the opening in the roof, and the two doors that also offered a lovely view outside. It was fitted out with a wood stove along the side, a big futon, a large chest of drawers, a small wardrobe, and a desk for the husband to work at, and there was still plenty of room for the baby to play with his toys.

Outside the husband had built a beautiful bathroom - you could lie in the bath and look at the stars - and a very sociable outdoor cooking/eating area. They had two fridges running on energy from twelve solar panels, several shelves to hold their produce, and a table and chairs to sit at. They even had a washing machine and recycled all their water by using it in the garden, and they had installed a huge underground tank to collect rainwater. On the sunny side of the kitchen he had ingeniously built a glass and wood conservatory to grow plants in.

FAREWELL

The time for me to leave was approaching. *'I have been here for five-and-a half weeks and it is time for me to leave this peaceful place and go back to Ibiza with a fund of knowledge. I am so lucky to have been able to learn all this information.'*

Just before I was due to go to Ibiza we had a beautiful day. We had a delicious meal at Es Ginebró Restaurant in Inca. This small vegetarian restaurant was serving delicious food, using all of the owner's own organic produce from their nearby smallholding. After we had eaten, we went picking blackberries before the leaving party that Natacha had organised for me that evening.

Friends arrived bearing goodies of all sorts. Someone brought pizzas; one guest brought delicious home-made vegan ice cream; a German restaurateur contributed a beautiful vegan cake; Natacha made a lasagne with polenta and, to quench our thirst she had made a variety of fruit drinks.

After we had eaten we all sat around enjoying a
musical get-together. Two of the men started
strumming their guitars while another sang. Then two
women joined in with the singing, and played their
drums. And all the while, as the music played, we
watched a lightening show in the distance. And then,
just as everyone was leaving at midnight, the much-
needed rains finally reached us. The timing couldn't
have been more perfect. It was a really beautiful
evening.

*'Tomorrow I leave early in the morning, Natacha will
take me to the ferry back to Ibiza.'*

chapter twenty three

Finding Land

When I got back to Ibiza I was finally able to make an appointment to meet the farmer that I had been told about the previous October - the farmer whose land I had been told I would be able to work.

' I am excited and a little apprehensive.'

I'd had a feeling that this was the land for me, and that there was a reason that I'd had to wait.

As I drove nearer, dark grey clouds were gathering in the sky. Perhaps, given the way things turned out in the end, I should have recognised this as an ominous warning.

Juan, the farmer turned out to be a small middle-aged Ibizencan who seemed to live on his own in a somewhat run-down finca. It was set in a small series of overgrown terraces banked up by dry stonewalls that seemed to be much in need of maintenance.

Even so, when I saw the land I felt as though I had found the perfect place. It was close to the sea, close to Santa Eulalia town, flanked on one side by woods and protected to the North by a mountain. And Juan seemed to be very happy to work with me following permaculture principles.

At that first meeting he told me that I would not be able to put up a yurt or a wooden house, as I had been planning to do, but that I could have a caravan. We arranged that I would go back the following Saturday to sign a contract, all brokered by Sonia who had originally found out that the land was being released for permaculture and who was also able to interpret for us. In my diary I noted, *'I am so happy.'*

But when I went back with Solara the following Saturday Juan had some bad news for me - I couldn't have a caravan. It seemed that the Ayuntamiento was having a purge and clearing caravans from the area, even where people had been living in them for a long time. This was despite a law stating that people working the land could have somewhere to live on that land. It appears that this is a law that loses the government money! Anyway, Sonia and the farmer were going to go to the Ayuntamiento to see what could be done.

'I went to see Juan today and he says the Ayuntamiento will not let me have a caravan, a wooden house or an earth ship, which would be good for the environment as it uses recycled materials. But amazingly I can build a house on 15,000 square metres of Juan's land. Never in a million years did I think this would happen, but I have been focusing on having land with a house. So happy with this turn around of circumstances! Juan is not charging me to rent the land. I will pay for the house and live in it for my lifetime. I will sign a contract with a lawyer to say I cannot be moved out of the house and that they will look after the food forest after I pass over. He and his son are very into nature. I think I have been sent to them. The Universe has planned it all in advance. There are a lot of hurdles to cross with the Ayuntamiento, with what you can and cannot do, but am visualising everything going smoothly. So now I am on hold again! Must be a reason.'

It would be a few months more before I understood that reason.

We started planning the house. Juan seemed to be as excited as I was. He started making drawings of the house and discussing with me what I would like. It would be an Ibizenco house, which has to face south. I was hoping to recycle all the water. I hoped to have a bath but, being conscious of the water shortages on the island, I don't have baths. However, if the water could be recycled it would be great. If I could get sponsored, I wanted to have a 100,000 gallon water tank to collect rainwater in case the wells ran out. And I also want to be completely off grid.

Juan asked me if he could help with the build, pointing out that this would mean that he would be able to keep an eye on the builders. I liked this idea as Natacha had had some builders working for her and they were always stopping for a smoke or on the phone or talking, and didn't get much done.

Juan seemed to want the house to be built quickly but six weeks later we still hadn't really got anywhere with the plans.

THE CRYSTAL GRID

Before I even got this land I had been channelled by Solara that there would be a ceremony to put a crystal grid on the land. Solara would open a portal and my frequencies would be put in the middle. Opening the portal would bring up new energies and make the fruit taste different.

'The chosen person/human that is by the name of Siriya has been chosen to open this part of the planet with the expression that she brings in. She is given the opportunity, the ease and the faculty to bring through the energy of my expression through the realm of earth and vegetable life, creating a garden of Light with bringing through the Divinity in the food that will be ingested, creating a healing through the Light that resides within.

Through the grid that you will be opening with the help of your sister Jade, you will be able to download and bring through the etheric crystals that need to be connected to that part of Earth. Jade will be aware and will be conscious of the coming down as crystal expression, but not recognising the energy in them as they are not from this planet.

It is a crystal bringing through the energy of the healing of the plants and vegetable realm. The crystals that exist upon the surface of Earth have this faculty but the ones coming from above are bringing new energy and Light expressions into the sphere of Earth. It is important to start doing this work, and not only here. You will be called to do this work in other places, as it will be known that the work is transforming the Earth at a different rate, vibration, and expression, allowing the growth to be accelerated. The harming products that have been used until now are not able to compete in that kind of progress. This progress is totally new. It uses other kinds of energies that reinforce in bringing Light to the earth and the seeds. It will bring Light energy in the flesh of all fruit and vegetable, transforming anybody that eats them, bringing Light through.

The crystal realm is eager to start functioning at this rate now. So all the crystals that will come forth in the Now, in etheric or physical ways, will all have this purpose. It is not the purpose of having a collection of crystals in your homes but to use them in this, bringing through these energies on Earth. The grids that have been formed until now are creating a similar work but in a mellower or softer way. Fusing with the etheric crystals propels the work and the intention. It brings forth a much more intensive vibration and energy in the growth and the earth. It is totally transformed in its structure.

The crystals have to be seeded, so to say, all around the land that Siriya is going to occupy and not only where the garden is going to be kept - in all its surface around it. It does not matter the size of the crystals. The etheric ones are four - one in each corner of the land and a major one in the centre. The physical ones are much smaller in size than the etheric ones. They are easier to bring through. They have to be mixed in between the etheric and physical ones to commune the energies and transform the crystals that reside within my body. It also transforms and heals the misuse of the crystals until now or too long time used as decoration or trophy for crystal hunters. The energies of the crystals within are going to change through the etheric ones now coming through. So you will be guided in every single seeding of crystal grids that are going to be opened on Mother Earth, as you have been guided until now.

The bringing down of crystal cities and etheric crystals will be in coordination of a Divine Plan guided by Light Beings from within and out of this plane and myself. All this to bring back the Glory of Gaia.

We thank you for being of service. These are important times and the celebration is here.'

Soon after that there was another channelling that called for a ceremony to be held within the next three weeks, before Solara's trip to India. I was told that it was a first ceremony and, for that reason, not to worry if there was a smaller group. The purpose was simply to initiate a crystal grid for the manifestation of the project in its highest form.

Jade, Aleteya and Jerimie would assist with the grid in different ways. Jeremie would have a particular crystal for the centre. We would make a small medicine wheel with crystals in the centre making a circle around the big main crystal, and there would be another set of crystals on the outside to mark the four directions of the compass. The blessings of each person present would be spoken and permission asked from the spirits of the land for the project.

Jade (Hippy Spirit) would show Aleteya how to make the crystal grid and Jeremie would have the correct crystal. If Aleteya had trusted she wouldn't have gone on a wild goose-chase to find the crystal for the centre. Jeremie had it all along.

Juan said he was up for the ceremony, and that he would like to be present and asked if he could take photos.

The day of the ceremony was scheduled for 1.11.2015 at 11a.m, just three years after my friend Hilary Carter had come to Ibiza to open a portal at Tanit's cave. I felt as though our journeys were entwined.

Aleteya and I went to cleanse the place a few days before the ceremony was due. We walked round the whole land and cleaned the area of bad energies with sacred sage. Then Aleteya was guided to the places where I should place the crystals. She was told the exact spot to put them and also the spot for the crystal grid.

My friend Christine phoned me and said she had missed her flight to France. She told me that she had never missed a plane before, so I said that it was probably because she was meant to be at the ceremony.

It was a beautiful day for the ceremony and eleven people attended. We stood in a circle while Solara cleared our auras with sacred sage. Then she asked the earth elementals - the wind, fire, and air - to come into the circle. We knelt on the ground and blessed mother earth, putting our intentions for the food forest into the crystal grid that Aleteya had prepared and activated and imagining how it would look. Then people spoke about how they felt about me making a food forest. All the while Juan was taking photos to record it.

As the ceremony drew to a close a huge bird of prey flew over the forest. Juan said it was unusual to see that particular bird. What a blessing, I thought - mistakenly.

chapter twenty four

Back at the Campsite

Now that I was back in Ibiza I reflected gratefully that I had been able to go to Mallorca for the height of the season. When I got back the mayhem that had begun before I left had really got underway and things seemed to be going from bad to worse.

By now a toilet seat that had been broken had just been left and not replaced. In the laundry both washing machines had stopped working, and the owner was refusing to have them put right. I felt sorry for young families having to do their washing in cold water.

As the season drew to an end things moved, once again, into a quieter time. It was interesting to watch the contrasting moods of the campsite as we went from spring promise through the madness of high summer with its left over debris, settling back, once again into a slower pace in autumn.

'It's now end of the season and people are beginning to pack up. The ones left are long term and more relaxed, and things are finally quietening down again. There were just two nights when they were playing their drums really loudly. It sounded as though they were in my caravan and lasted from 10 in the morning until midnight!'

'Even the owner is more relaxed now, even though there is a lot of clearing up to do. People who brought in mattresses, pallets, loungers and more have just upped and gone, leaving others to clear up for them. And then there is the one man who cleared everything, even the plants he had put in, and left it just as he had found it. He is a regular - comes every year.'

'This Cala Nova Camping site is lovely at either end of the season. There's a small pond with a fountain, and the sound of trickling water creates a feeling of calm while people relax on loungers, seemingly cocooned by all the plants around.'

On the 8th September we had terrific storms and torrential rain. Of course, this was the one time that I had forgotten to raise everything outside and put it onto the lounger or the table. Stepping out of the caravan onto my mat I found myself ankle-deep in water. Everything was soaked - my Spanish books, my beach blanket, my yoga mat - and my sandals, usually parked neatly at the bottom of the steps, were floating around anarchically.

The downpour had been so heavy that even my mattress in the caravan had become a bit wet. I was glad that I wasn't in a tent. Not surprisingly, a lot of people left after that rain. But the rain and thunder did a good clearing of the island.

MY BOOKS

I had written two books, *A Journey Beyond the Spirits* and *Divine Mystery,* about my global travels and spiritual evolution over the previous seven or so years, but was facing a few obstacles getting them printed and marketed. (I am due to re release them in the nest few months as the problems were never entirely resolved)

Now I met a young Dutch woman called Deike who was working hard to build a website called ibiza2love.com. It was to be a single internet stop bringing together information about all the many events, therapies, retreats and activities that the island has on offer, all under one umbrella.

She said she wanted to promote my books online with a view to eventually putting them up for sale on the site's web shop. I was pretty excited about it. Now she was offering to let me share her table at the Spirit Festival at Atzaró on October 4th. The Spirit Festival in Ibiza is a big gathering of people working with alternative therapies and spiritual practices that has gained a lot of momentum over the years, thanks to the tireless dedication of Sabina and Jerry Brownstein. It takes place in Spring and Autumn.

For a long time I had been unsuccessful in finding someone to print the books in Ibiza. Now, with just two weeks to go, Dieke had found someone who would print it and who was also prepared to design me a new cover for *Divine Mystery*. (I wasn't very happy with the cover that had been used on the first version of the book.) It was an extremely short deadline and I really had to trust the Universe that they would not only be printed but also delivered in time. Thankfully the man who took on the task was truly professional, worked hard and got it all done in time. My parcel of books arrived at the last minute, the afternoon before the Festival. I was as excited as a child at Christmas.

I sold twelve books at the festival - not bad for a first time.

On another occasion, when I was looking forward to a

chill-out day, Dieke rang me and asked if I would like to share her stall to sell my books at the Energy Week in San Antonio. The thing was, it was happening that very day. I had been very busy for the previous two days, moving all my trees and plants to the land at Juan's and was feeling tired. Nevertheless I decided that I couldn't keep giving in to tiredness, so I quickly packed my books into the car, made a picnic and set off.

During the longish drive across to San Antonio from Cala Nova realising just how tired I was feeling, I asked the Universe for someone to drive my car back for me. The tiredness began to feel overwhelming after a while on the stall, so I went to try and get some sleep on a bed under the trees. Deike kindly gave me a blanket, but sleep would not come. Then, as if by some miracle, Annika came by with a friend. Annika had shared my house for three weeks the previous year. When she saw how tired I was she offered to drive me home in my car with her friend following in their car.

'How I am looked after by just trusting.'

chapter twenty five

Winter Kicks In

I had found an apartment to rent for the winter.

It was a holiday apartment looking out onto the sea that I could have until March. I soon started to settle in.

'Pure luxury, to be ensconced in an apartment overlooking the sea. I have a washing machine and hot water - so great after washing by hand in cold water on the campsite. But I did enjoy outdoor living. I have a beautiful L-shaped settee with a piece jutting out, so I can put my feet up. You do appreciate things when you have not had them. I was so tired by the end of the day that I fell into bed for much needed sleep. In the morning I watched the sun rise over the sea. I can also watch the moon rise. Pure MAGIC.'

The following day the weather was horrendous, but it was spectacularly dramatic to watch from the apartment. It was like a tropical storm with high winds that churned the sea into huge waves and pounded them to the backs of the beaches and beyond. The waves hurled boats up, and onto the rocks where they smashed into splintered pieces, and the heaving waters spewed seaweed up onto the roads.

The heavy rain was certainly cleansing the land. People said it had been worse in 1969, but this was bad enough. Even so, they were glad of the water to fill their cisterns after two dry winters.

In spite of the weather I had to venture out to move the rest of my things from the campsite. The gate was locked when I got there, so I had to leave the car outside and keep going back and forth with armfuls of things. With every trip I had to brace myself from a wind that threatened to blow me over to the other side of the island. All the while the extension canopy on my caravan was flapping and slapping loudly with every gust, and I was certain that the wind would blow it away. Luckily it held firm.

I managed to take most of the things that day, so there was just one more day's work moving after that. Later in the week I went to clean the caravan and the carpet that I'd had outside, ready for Lyna who had bought it.

After that immense storm the weather was glorious for the next three weeks. The sea calmed again and I was able to swim nearly every day.

The last step in moving into the winter apartment in Es Canar was to collect the rest of my things from the garage at Sylvie and Mario's. The rain had got into that too, as it turned out.

'The garage has been flooded and my carpet got wet, and everything smells musty, especially any paper, so had to throw many paper things away. It's amazing how it seeps into everything. I had put dried sage from my garden in two jars and the sage smelt musty. I had to throw that away too. I washed the jars and they still smelt musty.'

'Now that the weather is hot and sunny, I can put things outside to air. A friend told me to put bicarbonate of soda on the carpet, leave it for a while, and then hoover the carpet. Apparently it will take the smell out.'

'I am now settled in for five months and who knows what the universe has up its sleeve for me then. Go with the flow!'

After that terrific storm my laptop was kaput. I managed for 25 days without one before I could meet

Andrea who had agreed to help me choose a new one. I had decided that I wanted to spend €500 on it and had drawn that amount of cash out to pay for it. As we walked into the shop I felt drawn to a red Acer that Andrea said was a good one. The price was €499!

A NEW ROLE

In December 2015 I went on a Tantra Course with Solara, staying at her house.

We started with a cobra breath initiation that Solara guided us through. It is the Tantra Kriya technique that has been transmitted verbally from Babaji through the lineage of Kriya teachers, and leads to a state of union with God.

We did a great deal of meditation to relax us and were taught how to forgive past relationships in our life. I thought I had forgiven my husband Gordon, but I found myself crying doing the work. Realising that I had not cleared it all I got rid of more "stuff," letting go to make way for a new partner to come into my life. We then had to imagine our new partner's higher self as light in front of us, and visualise linking each of our chakras with the partner's chakras by making a figure of eight to connect them.

We stopped for a delicious lunch that Ernesto had

prepared for us, and continued afterwards. Now we were to choose a partner from the group for the next activity. Then, for twenty minutes each, we stroked one another all over our bodies with just pure love.

Everybody in the group was channelled. As my channelling came at the end, they said:

> *"Siriya! Your energy field has opened threefold so that you are able to hold three times the amount of energy that you were holding previously. And this cannot be retracted. You cannot move backwards from this point so you will manifest even more easily than before because of your magnetic attractive field, providing you stay in good humour, good spirits and ever optimistic. The things that the Universe brings to you, each thing your heart desires, when it is appropriate that it shall be so and this is a blessing, is it not."*

There was a couple on the course both of whom were given new names. It was so beautiful to witness. They had got together during the last year and were told that they had a lot of work to do together. Ishtara was sung three times and Sananda was given his name.

Most of us were told that we would be doing different types of healing.

The next day we did a channelled meditation to open our hearts. We sat cross-legged opposite another person, touching each other, then looked into each other's eyes and gave love. The love went all round the circle. Those few days were very profound.

When the Monday dawned, the day that we were meant to leave, I did not want to go. Aleteya and Divyael were going to open a portal near Cala Llonga at midday and I asked if I could join them. When Milan, Sanandra and Ishtara also asked to join Solara said we were clearly all meant to go.

The portal was at the top of a sacred mountain that we had to climb. Reaching the summit, we came to the site of an ancient village, and a spot with fantastic views. Divyael held out his hands, feeling the energies for the right spot to clear. We all joined hands for the ceremony and were told that we had all been together in this place before. Earlier, when we had been climbing up, Milan had been holding my hand to help me up the steep mountain path. Later Sanandra said he thought Milan had been my son in a past life.

After that it seemed as though many people were being drawn to me to be helped. People were emailing me to tell me what an inspiration I had been to them. It was sometimes quite overwhelming trying to keep up with everybody. My book was also starting to help people. There was even one young woman who wanted to come to Ibiza to buy my book. I had met her at Solara's eighteen months earlier and had had a profound effect on her, she said.

I realised that this was now my new role.

chapter twenty six

Things Start to Unravel

All the while I was still waiting to start working the land at Juan's. Since the beginning of September 2015, for four-and-a-half months he had been going backwards and forwards to the Ayuntamiento, trying to sort out all the bureaucratic formalities.

In mid-January 2016 he had to start going through a large sheaf of letters written by his family that dated back to the 1800s. This was to confirm that the land did really belong to him. It was a long job. The handwriting of some of the letters was very small. Others had been written on watermarked paper, so that even with a magnifying glass they were difficult to read. The reasoning behind this was to confirm that ownership of the land had not been transferred to anyone else in the past – it seems that this often happened when people needed to pay off a debt. Finally, after many weeks it was all sorted out.

I arranged for Marcos to come and look at the land, as he had expertise in alternative building and permaculture. I had appreciated his advice on the land at the house in the campo, so I valued his opinion of this plot.

We had arranged to meet at 1p.m. Even though we both came early, we arrived at the same time. As I turned right coming from one direction, he turned left from the other direction. Pure magic! We walked around the plot and he told me that the land was good. The great news was that the rain run- off from the mountains and the road would water the trees so there would be no need to have swales.

Building a house on Ibiza turned out to be a much more complicated and expensive proposition than I had realised. Before you even start there are so many initial costs. For a start there are all the various taxes that the Ayuntamiento charge. Then there is the €2000 cost of drilling to find rock suitable for building on. When we eventually arranged a meeting with Juan, Sonia, the builder and me, he told us that we would have to wait for two years to divide the land. All the paperwork had to go to Palma for approval. By now the cost of building the house had gone up from

€120,000 to €135,000 – even before all the extras that would surely come up before it was done.

After all this, and with so much red tape to contend with, I decided I would not be having a house built and asked Sonia to tell Juan. I started looking for somewhere nearby to rent but I did wonder if she told him as he continued to look at articles about building with stone on the computer.

chapter twenty seven

Colour, Light, Energy, Dance

A channelling session with Aleteya brought messages from guides new to me.

'They tell me that around me there is a goddess with long blond hair, and many fairies working in the realm of colour. They tell me that wisdom resides in me from past lives with plants. WOW! I am also told to giggle a lot and not be serious.'

'You carry colour vibration. All the garden work you do brings magic. You bring colour and light; every single tree; the realm of vegetables. You have all the information within you; know directly. Plant something that is good for the tree to keep bugs away. Connection with wisdom and fairy world. Hear the vibration of plants: all plants are

an orchestra. Sit in a field of daisies and hear their vibration. Allow it to flow easier for communication. Tune in and sing with it. Become aware of what to heal within by sitting amongst flowers and trees. You are from another realm and you bring wisdom from it. We, the fairies and elementals from another dimension are very happy that you are part of this realm; that wisdom that you have dedicated, that expression on earth. Your connection is totally to Mother Earth. It is not necessary to connect to a higher vibration. Everything will come from Mother Earth.'

Aleteya is now talking in light language and I am crying. I think I remember speaking it on another planet. I have heard this language on the internet, so it is not such a surprise.'

"We have been waiting for this moment for a long time. You have been part of a long powerful project, started a long time ago, formed and reformed over and over. You did not belong here. You were on another planet, so you were called upon to bring your energy to this planet. Vegetable realm, all that is one, comes from your realm, your energy. You have come from other, divided into little parts of yourself and all is pure as you are. You are part of all the light

185

expression in colour and plants. You are not aware now as to where you come from - a necessary decision - you have forgotten. The energy you bring forth will be explosion energy. It has to be brought in gradually from many lifetimes. My gratitude to what you are bringing. I am always here if you are willing to work with me. I am honoured to work with you." Mother Earth speaking."

SHAMANIC DANCE

I never refuse an offer to go out, and I love dancing, so I was happy to accept an unexpected invitation to go to a blindfold dance. I had no idea what to expect and was filled with curiosity.

Diane picked me up and we drove up to a most beautiful location in the mountains. We entered a lovely large room with under- floor heating. What a godsend, in winter, to be nice and warm. A lady I knew was there too and told me that it was to be a shamanic dance ceremony. I was intrigued to know what we would be doing.

We were asked to sit cross-legged on cushions in a circle. We were eighteen people. Looking around I was surprised at how many young men there were in the group. Are they slowly waking up?

We began with a sage smudging. The Sacred Sage was

put in a dish and set alight then the dish was passed around the group. When it reached us we had to draw the smoke around our head and body with a feather to clear our auras of dark entities.

After that we stood up and put masks over our eyes. This was to help us to go inside ourselves. Now we were told to breathe through our noses. On each exhalation we had to bend our knees and say "HA" as we pushed the air out of our lungs to release blockages. We did this for five minutes, mindful of our intention while the energies were moving around our bodies.

Then we danced, trance-like, for an hour, just going with the flow of our bodies. The music was changing all the time. Nobody could see anyone else apart from the teacher who kept an eye on us to make sure we didn't bump into a wall or another person. Several people had amazing experiences. I didn't feel anything particularly and thought that might have been because I had already spent a lot of time cleansing myself of past traumas. I was told that something moves inside, even if we are not aware of it. In any event, I really enjoyed the evening and was grateful that I had been taken.

chapter twenty eight

I Turn Eighty

On February 10th, just a few days before my 80th birthday party at Solara's house, I recorded another synchronicity in my journal.

'Magical synchronicity today. I was going to go walking with Sheila but decided against it. I had slept badly and my son is coming tomorrow. I went to a nursery to buy two plants for Solara as she was going to let me have her house as a venue for my 80th birthday party. I had just arrived at the nursery and was looking at plants when my friend Sylvie came over to me. She had gone there to buy me a fruit bush and a Kaki (Persimmon) fruit tree for my birthday. I was able to take them straight to the land instead of her taking them home, then bringing them to the party and then me taking them to the land. I never cease to be amazed how

these interactions work from the Universe.'

The 14th February 2016 started with a bright blue sky and sunshine. I had known that my son and daughter-in-law were coming over from England for my birthday, but I was quite delighted when I discovered that my younger daughter had also come to surprise me! I hadn't expected that!

We had a great time with about 40 people. I had booked Greg Barry to do the catering. He made a mango lassi as a welcome drink and cooked a delicious Indian meal for us. We ended with four different cakes, all quite delicious. Greg had made a large cake with candles on it and Clare of "Oh So Bueno" had brought chocolate and carrot cakes and an unusual Bakewell Cheesecake.

Sarah was our disco girl. She had worked at Pacha when she first came to the island and was still working as a DJ, travelling sometimes to other countries. Now, she told me, she was finding it difficult. She could not cope so well with the changing energies.

It was amazing how I had met Sarah. I had been thinking of asking Solara if she knew anyone who could do the disco for my party. Then, when I went to help with a group of youngsters doing permaculture, Sarah came and sat next to me and asked if she could come to my party. I said, "Yes," then she told me that she was a DJ and offered to play for me free of charge. What a lovely young woman! I was thrilled. I believe that she was sent to me.

The music she chose was great, and everyone danced enthusiastically and had lots of fun. All without alcohol!

chapter twenty nine

Things Go Pear-Shaped

The situation with the land was as yet, unsettled, but as far as I knew they were still in train.

'Really have to trust as it's now March 21st and I still have not heard anything, but am focusing on the house and price.'

The time was drawing near for me to leave my winter-let apartment in Es Canar and I needed somewhere to move to.

I arranged for Sonia, who was working for APAEEF (Association Productus Agricultura Ecologica Elvissa), to come along to a meeting with Juan so that we could discuss the contract and my ideas. She brought drawings of what I had in mind for the land - a garden area round the house, with permaculture vegetables around that. Beyond that there would be an area planted up with 200 trees, a wildlife pond with a solar-driven fountain (moving water keeps mosquitoes away), and another area strewn with wild flowers to attract bees and butterflies.

Things seemed to be shaping up nicely. *'Hope to sign a contract in two weeks with Banco De Terres.'*

Around that time a young man John, like me also passionate about permaculture, came into my life to help me and I him. I showed him where to get caña, something that grows everywhere on Ibiza and is similar to bamboo. I used it for training plants like tomato and cucumber. John cut it down while I stacked it. The pieces were so long that they were hanging out of the back of his van. On the drive back I had to sit on the floor in the back with the caña. Luckily we were not stopped by the police.

Later he invited me to see what he was doing on a piece of land that he had permission to work. He had worked very hard, bringing in much soil, mulch and straw. He'd made beds where he'd planted 50 raspberry and 50 blackberries plants, and covered the ground around the plants with straw. He was going to create a pond for wildlife and make a chill-out area surrounded by flowers. He was fortunate in having avocado trees full of flowers as well as avocados on the bushes, so he would get an extended fruiting season.

I went for a channelling with Ernesto and was told that I must keep on writing my book. 'It does not matter if it is not perfect.' I was also told that my guides were trying to bring Juan's energies up to a level with mine.

On Monday March 22nd everything went pear shaped.

After waiting for six months I finally got the contract for the land. There were ten clauses. Not one of them was good for me.

I could not rent the land, so Juan would be in control and could come onto it whenever he liked. He could pick any existing fruit on the land. Not only that, he also wanted to be able to take fruit and vegetables for all his family. There would not be much there anyway for the first few years, so I wouldn't have been able to be self-sufficient. Finally, there was a clause that stated that, when I could not manage it any more, I would have to leave.

I was so upset. I had thought he was a nice man when I first met him. He seemed to change as time went on.

'What an unfeeling man! Just out for what he could get from me! I would be his slave! No way would I sign the contract! I was hoping to plant next week and had potted up many daisy plants to make a flower

meadow. I had put in cuttings of Siempre Verde, an evergreen plant for hedging. I was all ready to go.'

'Now I have had enough of watering my plants in pots. It has gone on for a year. I have driven all over the island to water my plants! I will give the plants to my good friend John who has just acquired some land and wants to plant fruit trees. I know they will be in good hands.'

Between three of us, with three vehicles – John with his car, a friend with a big van and me with my car - we managed to move all the trees and plants to John's land in one day. The next day, when I went with my friend to collect some more of my things - a table, the Kaki tree that Sylvie had given me for my birthday and a shrub for bumblebees - I was shocked to see that everything had gone except the compost that I had been collecting. John offered to come with me to see what had happened to everything. Juan's story was that someone must have stolen everything! It was clearly he that had done the stealing! Nothing had been taken before, and it was funny that it was just the day after I had started collected my things that everything disappeared. I lost two compost makers, a cold frame, a table, two plants, and a few other odd things.

John's wise advice was, "Just let it go and keep away as

far as you can from this man. He will get his just desserts tenfold for what he has done." Even so, it was hard to put his advice into practice. I was deeply disappointed and very angry.

'It's really surprising on this island. Nobody wants you to plant fruit trees on their land. Such a challenge when one is trying to help the planet. The council stops you at every turn. You cannot live on the land that you are working. I have been feeling very down. Apparently the planets were in alignment and affecting everybody. The lady next door could not take all the energies and went back to Holland. Many people are saying they are waking at 3a.m, myself included. It has been a very difficult two weeks. It's not easy living on this island with some Ibizencan people. I heard of a friend who rented a house for a year. She made a beautiful garden and was then told to leave. I find this very sad.'

Back at the apartment I had a minor accident after that. I had been packing a case and left it open at the bottom of the bed. When I stretched over it to reach my work basket and then sat back on the bed I missed the bed and fell off the end. I hit my head on the floor and hurt my elbow and neck. As I lay there doing Reiki on my head I asked, 'What is going on?'

After that things seemed to get better. Perhaps I knocked some sense into my head! I decided to cheer myself up by watching Mooji, a guru who gives Satsang. The two people who had come to him were in fits of laughter for the whole interview. It really made me feel good.

Then I had a nice surprise - a phone call telling me that I could stay in the apartment for another month. That gave me time to manifest another house.

chapter thirty

Shifting Energies

We had been told that the energies were going to be very strong in April and advised not to look at too much internet.

On the 10^(th) March I went to help John plant up some shrubs on his land.

We worked for three hours in the sun before I drove home to my apartment. That evening, at about 9 o'clock, I started to feel dizzy. I wondered if it could be ascension symptoms, so I went to bed. The next day I felt really weird, and could not sit up without feeling dizzy and being sick.

Fortunately I had read on the internet that this could happen otherwise it could have been scary. All that day

I could not eat and had difficulty drinking water, and the following day I felt drained of energies. However, I did manage to get up to make a smoothie and later on I mustered up enough energy to prepare a small amount of cauliflower cheese for my meal. I was still feeling some dizziness, but it wasn't so bad.

My neighbour told me I needed to go to hospital, and another lady said I should go and get some pills from the pharmacy. People are so conditioned to immediately rush to the doctors at the slightest problem. My answer to both of them was: "I know what this is and hospital is the last place I would go and, besides, taking pills just slows down your ascension."

There were so many energies coming into my head. I knew something big was happening. I knew that the right thing to do was to rest up in bed, with no internet or phone. I knew the tiredness I was feeling would pass. I could feel a lot happening to the right side of my head and eye, and it took some time for the dizziness to pass, so I couldn't drive anywhere for quite a while. But after two weeks I was feeling back to normal.

One morning, when I woke up before the sun came up, I looked out at the early morning sky. There, hanging in the sky, was a spaceship. I had wanted to see another one for some time, so I sat and watched it until, after gradually getting smaller and smaller, it disappeared. I wondered if something had been done to enable me to see one now.

MANIFESTING SUMMER LODGINGS

I was due to leave the apartment on May 1st and, having a strong feeling something would turn up in time, I had been manifesting a house with two bedrooms. Then I realised that that wasn't going to happen for the price I could afford, so I surrendered everything and imagined the wall of a house with a large €600 written on it. This is how I manifest. Even so, one friend looked dubious when I told her this is what I was doing - the prices in Ibiza in summer were ridiculous.

By the time I had to move I still hadn't found anywhere. Fortunately Solara had told me that I could stay at her house while I joined two of her retreats. So that is where I moved, with all my goods and chattels from the apartment in Es Canar - rugs, lamps, books, chests of drawers, bedside tables, crystals, kitchen ware.... and, of course, plants! Luckily I could put some things into my room and there was space in some of the outhouses to store bigger things. Outside and in the garden there were plenty of places for me to keep my plants. Moving everything took several trips, even with plenty of help, but finally I was able to settle again for a while, and take time to get grounded again.

The retreat was the perfect place for me to be after the move. I could relax totally in a group of people that I gelled with immediately. There were four other participants - two from Holland, Suan and Iris, and Emma and Maxine from England. We worked on our chakras, meditating in nature and, on one special day, bringing in codes from other dimensions.

Emma told me about a lady who had started yoga at 74 years of age and, at 104 years young, she is more flexible than some of the other students. She rarely misses a lesson and picks up a 60-year old friend to take her to the class in her little yellow mini car. What an inspiration! We are never too old to do things and this keeps us fit and healthy.

One evening we all went to Es Vedra for a meditation and a picnic watching the sunset. Several other people had congregated to watch the sun go down. And it was magnificent with beautiful colours around it - purple at first, then emerald green with olive green in the centre - magical!

During the first week of the retreat my friend Aleteya asked me if I had found a house. When I said, "Not yet," she told me she had a friend with an apartment to rent for the summer. I imagined that it would be in a block with just a terrace for my plants.

Imagine my delight when I went to look at it, and discovered that it was a small, one-bedroom casita surrounded by beautiful gardens. Not only that. Compared to the apartment I had just left, it was very spacious - and I could grow my vegetables on a plot right next to the house. And the price was €650, inclusive of the water! (I had been paying €50 a month for water at the previous place anyway, so the place that I manifested was exactly what I had imagined.) It was near the sea at Cala Llonga, and also close to Santa Eulalia. And the eco farm where I buy organic produce was also very close by.

Nine days before I had to leave Solara's I had found the perfect casita. Interestingly, it had been just nine days before I'd had to leave the campsite that I had found the apartment in Es Canar. When things like that happen it makes me trust completely.

When Solara came to look at it with me, her surprised comment was, "This is just you!" I think she was looking at the purple colour on the walls - I always wear purple - but everything else suited me perfectly too. I had permission from the owner to grow vegetables the permaculture way.

SOUL FAMILY

The second of the retreats at Solara's was totally different from the first. Again there were four other people so, including Solara and me, we were six. The other participants were Inge and Ishtara from Holland, Corine from Spain, and Christine who had come from Kuwait where she lives with her Egyptian husband.

On the first evening Solara told us that we would be channelled, and that there was an energy connection in each of us, and that we are a soul port.

'We have been called to do a visualisation of energy. You are a glowing ball of light frequencies. Move into the experience now from every vortex of light within you. Become bright white light, an organic ball of frequency. Now there is a line between each one of you creating a dodecahedron. When you sit in a circle, you are a united energy field, a union of divine energy. Project this glowing frequency in perfect harmony into the centre of your circle for fifth dimensional earth, all in an octahedron, sending light frequencies to the world to bring light, joy and peace. This is your soul purpose. We are activating an ascension grid around the planet.'

I felt so blessed to be part of this work.

I was told that my soul family is attracted to me now, so I can assist them and they can assist me. We are a soul family from the same place; the second chakra connects us.

We were told that we had some homework to do. I was told that my heart is open and flowing, but that I had to let go of pain and defences. I had to concentrate on my aura now and focus on above and below, front and back, side to side once a day, moving towards making myself invisible to any enemies. When we are light workers the dark are trying to stop our work, so our task is to clear the dark entities.

I was channelled that, although I had lost the land at Juan's, the crystal grid that we had put on it would have affected the farmers in the surrounding area. I was also told that Juan is crying in his subconscious because, by being too greedy, he lost the land being used well. Even so, the whole episode will have changed him. In the meantime, three people have told me that I will get some land before the end of the year

chapter thirty one

Another Move

After the two retreats Mary Lynne, Christine and Ernesto helped me with yet another move. We loaded up three cars with furniture, books, rugs, heaters, plants and compost as well as suitcases and boxes filled with clothes and foodstuffs, and wound our way, in convoy, through the campo on the back roads and along dirt-tracks.

Arriving at the gates to the property, we tried again and again to unlock them - without success. Phone calls to several people proved fruitless - no-one was answering. Ernesto needed to go on to work, so we juggled the contents of all the cars around a bit so that he could drive away with slightly less baggage in his car for now. He would return with the rest of the stuff later.

While we were waiting for someone to return my calls, we three women set off for a bite to eat down in Cala Llonga. It was the perfect solution. We were all hungry. Of course, during the meal I received a text message explaining that the lock to the gate was broken and that it would be open when we went back!

It was a relief to be able to move things into the house.

'Settling into my new home is a joy. The first thing to do is get the vegetable patch ready. It was hard work collecting the compost and seaweed that I had stored at Solara's. I asked Milan for help and he kindly came to move some of the compost, then he helped me to prepare the garden by digging some beds ready for planting. We laid the compost on top. The next day, in great excitement, I went to buy some organic vegetable plants from a new outlet that a friend had recommended to me. It was too late to grow from seed by now. They had a wonderful selection - many varieties of tomato, beetroot, several types of melon, watermelon, lettuces, peppers, leeks.... Loaded up with all these goodies I made my way home to plant them.'

On the way I called into a Ferreteria (hardware shop) to buy a nozzle for the hose. As I entered the shop I noticed that the time on my phone was 12.12. When the shopkeeper told me the price was €5.55 I felt compelled to ask, amazed, if that was correct, scarcely believing her until she showed me the bill. Later that day I looked at my phone again and it was 21.12. It was going to be a good day.

'I am so happy in my new house, enjoying every moment until end October when I have to leave. But you never know what is round the corner.'

A SURPRISE FAMILY VISIT

Towards the end of May my daughter Heather told me that she might come over from Germany for a day one Wednesday. I had no internet, so our only connection was by phone. Nothing had been confirmed so I was most surprised to suddenly get a text message the Sunday before she had said she was coming, asking me if I could meet her at the bus station in Es Canar at 2 o'clock.

As I hugged her, this strange, hunched man wearing dark glasses and a hat pulled right down over his eyes came up to us and insistently asked where he could find a toilet. In the end he said, "I need to go now! I'm going to mess my pants!" Thinking he was a bit mad, I said to my daughter, "We need to get away from this man!" At that point he said "Hello Siriya," and I realised that the weird man was, in fact, my son-in-law.

He'd come as a surprise to me. When they told me that they would be staying for a week I changed all my plans for the time they were here. It was lovely.

We explored some of the island together. Walking through some beautiful countryside one day we stopped for lunch at the beach restaurant at Cala San Vincente. It was much improved from the previous year, with wide seats and the roof covered with palm fronds, and a great place to chill out in the heat.

Their last day started off a bit fraught. We'd had a few problems meeting up when they'd missed the bus from Es Canar and I couldn't find my phone. Back at my house in Cala Llonga I asked the angels to help me find my phone. When I told my neighbour Inge my problem, she offered to call it. It started to ring - in the bathroom - not a place where I normally had it. I was mightily relieved, because I normally have it turned off.

So, in the end all worked out fine and Heather, John and I had a fabulous last day together enjoying the icing on the cake - a trip to La Paloma in San Lorenzo, which is a super place to eat. Sitting under dappled shade from orange trees, we had a magnificent view across to the mountains on a beautiful day before they left again.

VEGETABLES AND WILDLIFE

Back at the apartment everything was delightful.

'The vegetable patch is coming on a treat. While I was watering the ground to let the water seep into the beds, a little bird was flitting round the olive tree in front of me. I was trying to see what it was and silently asked, "Will you come closer so that I can see you clearly." Suddenly the little thing flew down right under my feet and had a bath in the water. It was a beautiful Goldcrest. Such a joy! And the thought crossed my mind that I had been communicating telepathically with the bird.'

The next night while I was watering two birds came in the tree.

'I am having some problems with rabbits. They are eating my melon plants, lettuces and the leaves of the small beetroot. They don't seem to touch them when they are bigger, thankfully. I've decided to grow vegetables that they don't eat.'

'Inga, who lives next door, wants to learn permaculture, so she has dug some beds and is growing a few vegetable plants. But the soil there was dry and hard, so I taught her how to mulch to keep the sun off the soil and to hold the moisture in and showed her the difference between her patch and mine, which is well covered with seaweed. There wasn't enough of

the seaweed that I had already collected for her beds too, but we did eventually go to get some more and she is happy with the outcome.'

chapter thirty two

Kundalini Yoga

'It is fast approaching the end of June. My Chilean friend, Sonia, whom I got to know when I was staying on the campsite in Cala Nova, is starting a small business combining yoga on the beach with an organic detox breakfast. She is trying to promote her food. Suan, who is staying next door with Inge, said she would take me along as she is interested in learning a new type of yoga. Very unusually it was raining a little, but in the end the six of us in the group were able to have our class anyway. Our teacher was a beautiful Italian young woman called Ria. She was teaching us Kundalini Yoga. It was very powerful.'

'The detox breakfast afterwards was prepared by Wendy, who has been a chef on Ibiza for many years and specialises in raw food. She comes from England *originally but has lived on Ibiza for 30 years. She told us how, when she first came to the island, you were allowed to climb the rock of Es Vedra. She was young then, but still it took three hours to climb. They found a flat place to put up a tent and spent the night there. It must have been amazing. There were blue lizards there that are not seen anywhere else in Ibiza. Then she told us that there is a cave under the rock and when she swam into it she felt as though she was in another world, and was blown away by the energies. It certainly is a special place. Sadly all that has been stopped now and people are not allowed on the rock.'*

I have recently started practising Kundalini Yoga with a radiant and calm teacher, a young woman called Ria. This is the story of how she came to be in Ibiza after a pivotal moment that changed her life.

RIA

"I was in my home town in Italy, starting the third year of my PhD in Evolutionary Biology. Since a couple of years I had started to feel a crisis arising in me, a sense of contraction and limitation. Suddenly that feeling started to be stronger, almost unbearable.

I had a boyfriend at that time. He was very wealthy. I could have had anything I wanted. His family had just bought a house for us and we were going to live together very soon. But there was a voice inside me getting louder and louder asking for freedom, inner seeking, breaking the rules, and exploring life. One day I thought, "Nobody is going to change my life. Only I myself have to change it. What am I waiting for?" It was very hard for me, because I really loved my boyfriend. He had a very good heart. He was in a crisis too. It was related to his family and job. He was telling me all the time that I was the only reference point for him. Soon he started to go to a psychiatrist, and taking drugs. I was feeling a strong responsibility for him. I was carrying it all on my shoulders.

After not sleeping for a month I decided I could not be a reference point for him if I couldn't be a reference point for myself. I was losing my centre and inner balance. So I decided to start a new chapter of my life and be alone, free to find myself, and my purpose in life.

I went to visit Anna Lisa, a dear friend of mine who was living in Barcelona. As I arrived an inner sense of freedom was vibrating in me. I was feeling alive, happy and excited about everything I was experiencing. As the time to go back to Italy came closer an internal feeling of sadness started to arise in my body. Fears, worries and doubts became overwhelming. Shall I really do it? Shall I really do it until the end and follow this voice inside me? I postponed my flight to gain some perspective on my feelings. I couldn't ignore them. The answer was there, clear in my body and clear in my feelings.

When I went back to Italy I started to tell everyone that I was going to leave everything - job, PhD course, and home town - to move to Barcelona. Most of the people thought I was crazy to leave my career at the University and a secure life, for a dream. But nobody could convince me of the opposite.

It was really a jump into the void after having everything safe and secure. But life teaches us that the greatest challenges bring the greatest opportunities. Somehow new doors started to open up on my way. My professor at the Italian University, who really believed in me, found a laboratory at the University of Barcelona where I could finish my PhD course. I was very happy to be able to change my life and still conclude the previous chapter of it. I've always loved science but it simply wasn't enough to respond to my internal quest.

One day in Barcelona my spiritual mother (she is my father's wife and my brother's mother) sent me an email. She wrote, "Look for yoga in Barcelona." I did not pay to much attention to those words as I was in a hurry to see an apartment. At that time I was sharing a one-room apartment together with Anna Lisa. We were sleeping together in a double bed. When we were hanging clothes to dry in the small entrance, which was also the kitchen, corridor and living room, it was almost impossible to walk into the house! We really needed to find a new place! So I quickly left the house.

I was walking fast down the street with the new apartment in my mind...... How would it look? Would it have a balcony? Would there be space enough to invite friends? I was so immersed in my thoughts that there was no space for anything else...

Suddenly I felt a very strong energy around me and I had to turn my head to see what was there capturing my attention in such a moment of un-presence! SHUNIA YOGA I could read above the entrance of what looked like a Yoga Centre. Immediately I remembered the email and that sentence from my spiritual mother. I didn't even have to look for it! It came to me! The feeling that I had to go inside was too strong to go back to thinking about the new apartment. As I got inside the feeling that "everything will fall into place" was arising deeply in my heart. I was in the right place at the right moment. I asked if I could try a class, because I had never practised Kundalini Yoga. "Come tonight" they told me. And so I did. It was a Kundalini Yoga class for women. It was so magical. All these women wearing white clothes, smiling to each other and really happy to be there. We were moving all together, keeping our eyes closed. We were looking inside of ourselves but still keeping the connection to the group, listening to our breath and chanting mantras. "This is my tribe," I felt. And from that moment I practised every single day, ether in the centre or on my own. After a couple of weeks I already knew I wanted to do the teacher training. It was just My Thing.

That time in Barcelona was very intense. During the day, I was studying and writing my PhD thesis. I was going to yoga classes, practising by myself and studying for the teacher training. At night, I was working as a waitress in an Italian restaurant to make a living. Once summer arrived I started to practice in a small green area outside the restaurant before going to work. People passing by started asking me if I could teach them yoga. Also a few friends of mine who were working with me started to ask me for classes. Very soon I had built up a small group of students and I also started to give regular Kundalini Yoga classes. It's amazing how much energy the Universe was giving to me!!! Clear sign that I was on the right path! When you serve the Universe and follow your path, the Universe starts to serve you!

One year later, a flyer advertising a European Kundalini Yoga Festival fell into my hands. I didn't need to look at the description or check the price. I just knew that I had to go. It didn't matter what that meant; I had to go. I put together all the money I had to go to France. I decided to leave the job in the restaurant - they wouldn't have given me holidays in the middle of the high season in August. I wanted to go and feel free to flow with the Universe, going where life wanted to take me.

I remember my Kundalini Yoga teacher at that time explained to me that three days of the eight-day long festival consisted of White Tantric. White Tantric is part of Kundalini Yoga. It is a group meditative practice that works on clearing out the deepest corridors of the subconscious mind. One day of White Tantric consists of 6 - 8 meditations of 31 or 62 minutes, with short breaks in-between. White Tantric is practised in pairs. Men and women sit along different parallel lines facing each other and follow the instructions of the Tantric facilitator, who represents the Mahan Tantric Yogi Bhajan.

I remember my teacher telling me, "Don't do the white tantric with the same guy for the three days otherwise you are going to fall in love!" I looked at her and these few words came out of my mouth without me realising it, "I know that I am going to fall in love, that's why I am going!" I was astonished by what I had just said. I looked at her, and we both started to laugh.

I remember that, inspired by what had just happened, before leaving I wrote a letter to the Universe specifying the main features that the coming guy had to have: good looking, smart, loved travelling, already on a spiritual path. I could learn from him. He was not Italian. Possibly came from a country where I didn't know the language. He played an instrument and loved dancing. He could practice Kundalini Yoga with me and we could grow together on this path. Wahe guru! And so I left Barcelona; direction Fondjouan in the South of Paris.

I hardly knew anyone at the Festival but I felt at home. It was a feeling of being in a community based on love, sharing and supporting each other. The routine in the days before White Tantric was pretty intense. The diet and the schedule were designed to prepare us for the three days of White Tantric: we woke up at 3.45 a.m. for Sadhana (morning yoga practice) then went to the Gurdwara (temple) to chant mantras; served breakfast, ate breakfast; went to Misseling (regular meeting with all the people who talked your language); workshop in the morning; Masterclass at lunch, dinner; workshop in the afternoon; evening yoga class. For sure by 9 p.m.

you just wanted to see your bed and could sleep beautifully, even on the hard, uneven tent floor.

During these days people look for their partners for the three days of White Tantric, and most of the guys (in a minority with respect to the girls) are usually fully booked. Well, the day before the Tantric arrived and I had no partner yet. A few guys had asked me but they were simply not *him*. Somehow I was feeling so happy and fulfilled at the festival that I was super relaxed about not having found my partner yet. I trusted the plan of the Universe and enjoyed my freedom to be able to flow with it very much.

In the evening of that day I went to a Laughing Yoga workshop. I was a bit tired but I knew the teacher and he insisted that I go. We were playing many different games that all ended up with laughing. There were two guys who were capturing my attention. They were laughing very loudly and trying without success to get a smile out of a group of very serious Chinese girls. At a certain moment we played a game where we were supposed to find a random partner in the group, exchange a Mudra (yogic hand position) and then laugh together. It was making no sense but that was the beauty of the game - to laugh without a reason. After laughing we were to change partners again. I remember when, at one point I coupled with one of those two funny guys. We looked into each other eyes and, while laughing, he stumbled and fell right in front of me. We laughed even more. I loved the easiness and tranquillity with which he stood up again with a big smile, making fun of himself. We smiled at each other and then switched partners again.

The workshop came to an end and I left to have a walk around the lake. At a certain point I saw the same guy looking at me. He smiled. I smiled and he joined me. He introduced himself as Bachittar, a spiritual name meaning Warrior of Light. We started to talk about science and spirituality, Kundalini Yoga, travelling..... I was very surprised by the width of interests and expertise of this very good-looking German yogi. "Was he the one I was waiting for?" I thought about my list of my dream man and I thought: "Wow! I just got to know him and we are already getting very close!" He asked if I had a partner for the following day of White Tantric and very happily I said that I was free. He told me that he had already reserved a spot, right in front of the stage... a very privileged spot!!! As a very gentle man he invited me to see the spot where we would meet next morning. Something magic happened. As he was showing me the place, he gently touched my lower back. I had goose bumps everywhere and felt a spiral of energy rising up my spine. "It's *him*!" It was very challenging to contain the energy that I immediately felt in my body.

After showing me the place we greeted each other and left to go to sleep and recharge for the next day. When I was sure he couldn't see me any more I started to jump, run and open my arms to the sky...it's him!!!! It was quite late already, considering that we had to wake up at 3.45 in the morning. Well, I danced for the next two hours feeling like a Goddess...everybody was looking at me. I was feeling sensual and beautiful as I had never felt before. When the music finished I went to the tent with my mind telling me that I HAD to sleep. But, if I slept one hour that night it was a lot. I had so much energy and I was so happy that I couldn't close my eyes.

Next morning, super excited, I went to the big tent where the White Tantric was taking place. I started practising some warm up exercises waiting for Bachittar, but he wasn't there. Almost all couples had already formed and nobody was sitting in front of me and no one was sitting in front of the guy who was sitting to my left. I knew from my feelings that Bachittar wasn't there because something had happened.

White Tantric was going to start. The guy beside me who was a friend of Bachittar's (I found out later) looked at me and I looked at him and we decided to do the first meditation together while we waited for our respective partners. At the end of the first meditation Bachittar arrived. His phone had been stolen from his tent, together with his wallet and credit card. He was very shaken. He had had to take the time to call his bank in Germany to block the cards. When he saw his friend sitting in front of me, he said: "Please, I just lost everything I had in my tent. Please at least leave me my girl." The other guy looked at me and said: "You know what you are asking me, my friend. Look at her! I will only agree as you are my friend, and I love you." And our journey together started, falling more and more in love after each meditation.

During the following months we travelled between Barcelona and Germany, and then we went to Canada to work together on a consciousness project spreading yoga, meditation, breathing and other consciousness techniques. We were happy together but already facing the first challenges in our relationship, from which we were both learning a lot. His tendency was to be very dominant and space-taking, and my response to his attitude was to make myself very small and powerless. I was a completely different person compared to the determined, intuitive and dynamic girl I was when I was single. I was seeing him as smarter, faster, and stronger and I was, partly unconsciously, giving up my power as a woman.

In our relationship we have consciously decided to go through these challenges. We talk a lot and practice Kundalini Yoga to improve ourselves, to refine our mind patterns, to solve blockages and to go through our personal issues. We have ended up learning and growing a lot together. He is learning to contain his energy, to respect me as a woman and to give me space. For my part, I am learning to hold my power in his presence, stand up to him if I need to, find my inner confidence and trust in myself. Our relationship has become uplifting and magical in so many aspects and it's beautiful now to see our love growing on a strong foundation of mutual esteem, respect and trust.

Our project with our Canadian friend was over and we were in the process of deciding where to go and where to settle for a while…. Europe, Central America, Australia… we contemplated all these possibilities. One morning in Montreal, after our yogic morning practice, Bachittar told me he'd had a vision of us on Ibiza. He had been to Ibiza. I had not, but somehow I felt a very pleasant feeling in my body as he shared his vision. We decided to leave the decision open to be able to feel and contemplate more about it.

A couple of minutes later I picked up a Canadian magazine left around by our housemate and opened it randomly. Astonished, I stared at the page. There was a photograph of beautiful landscape of the island and IBIZA written in capital letters. I ran to tell Bachittar, "This is the sign! The sign from the Universe! We have to go to Ibiza!!!" And so we did.

Back in Europe we attended a Kundalini Yoga training called "The 21 Stages of Meditation." We were so connected to ourselves and to each other after the training that we decide to use that deep inner connection to manifest our dream. We wrote and drew on a piece of coloured paper how we imagined our life on Ibiza would be. We called in the angels, sent prayers, and asked for higher support from the Universe. Right after that we went to Ibiza to visit the island.

As soon as I got off the plane I felt the powerful energy of the island. Then, during Sadhana, our Kundalini Yoga early morning practice, I had the most powerful experience. I was feeling the Earth supporting me, holding me, and giving me energy. I was feeling received and loved by the land. It was the most beautiful experience of Mother Earth that I had ever felt so strongly in my body. After a month we were already settled on the island.

My financial resources were almost at zero when I arrived, as I had spent most of my savings travelling and learning. I felt some fears and worries arising in me. I was starting a life from zero. But I said, "Yes! This is the moment and I am going to manifest my dream." I really put all my love and passion into teaching and into my dream to spread the techniques that had changed my life from the inside out. I'm happy and grateful to see, day by day, this dream come true."

And that is Ria's story so far. Somehow it worked out. She is beginning to get known now as an excellent teacher, I think she will go far.

chapter thirty three
Summer Hibernation

Through going to the Yoga I was invited to go to a beautiful Tibetan singing bowl meditation that is held at Es Vedra every week. We each had a crystal put on our third eye at the start of the session. While the singing bowls were being played I felt a soreness on the left side of my head for some time. Jeremy, who was running the meditation, said it was probably something being moved by the vibration of the music.

On July 3rd Inge invited me to Santa Eulalia to a musical jam, where musicians who have not played with each other before make music together.

'There were two girls singing with the band. It was so beautiful. I danced for two hours to guitar music after swimming in the sea. We walked back along the

promenade to the car, listening to the sound of the waves on a balmy evening, looking up at a star-filled sky.'

'Last week I swam at Cala Llonga and was stung by a jellyfish. There are many more than there used to be around Ibiza; several different kinds. People are unaware that turtles eat jellyfish, but the turtles are dying because of people's thoughtlessness. The plastic bags that are carelessly abandoned and end up in the sea are causing the problem. The turtles eat them thinking they are jellyfish. When they are found dead their stomachs are full of plastic. It is so very sad.'

'During July and August in Ibiza, when the roads and towns are busy with all the tourists around, I just stay at home. I could not have wished for a better place to be than in this casita. The sea is nearby for a late evening swim after all the tourists have left the beach. Can Muson, the organic farm with fresh fruit and vegetables is nearby. I buy in and stock up on food so that I don't have to go in to town. I love these two months.'

'So, I feel many changes in my body during this time and I'm finding that I need to sleep a lot. I think I made the right decision to take time out. In front of the casita there is concreted-over swimming pool that creates a perfect space for yoga and meditation in the shade of

the early morning sun. I've laid down a plastic carpet to cover the concrete and my Buddha presides over us there, with crystals and shells decorating the floor at his feet. In the late morning an orchestra of cicadas starts singing, in waves; first one, then gradually the noise rises to a crescendo all around the garden and from the surrounding woods. Sitting quietly you hear the sounds of nature. It is never still. Leaves are falling; bark is dropping from the tree trunks; the birds are singing. I am really enjoying my time here in this magical place.'

I thoroughly enjoyed staying at home in my beautiful casita and garden, meditating for the earth and people on it, until the beginning of September, when I would start going into town again.

chapter thirty four

Mallorca, Summer 2016

I wanted to go back to Mallorca to see Natacha again. I decided to go in September and had found a vegetarian Bed and Breakfast where I could stay in the mountain village of Soller. When I tried to book in for the 14th they told me that their only available dates were from the 24th to 29th. I had planned to stay with Natacha for part of my stay and didn't know if this would fit. Once again, though, even this apparent setback turned out for the best. When I finally heard back from her she told me that the 14th would be the perfect day to go to hers. Her birthday was the 15th.

I was going to take the night ferry across from Ibiza to Mallorca, and had arranged for a lift to the ferry port with Edward. As we neared the ferry terminal I felt as though I was being given a most beautiful send off -

the sky was aflame in the setting sun and the evening clouds were infused with a rich, deep pink.

There was no queue at the ticket office. The girl on the desk spoke excellent English. The price of the return ticket to Palma was €105. It all seemed so much easier than booking online. We had a smooth crossing and I was able to lay down and nap for the three and a half hour journey.

Natacha was waiting outside the terminal for me when I arrived at Palma. It was so great to see her again. We drove through the night for half an hour until we reached her rented house near Caimari.

My senses were flooded with delectable sensations as I stepped out of the car when we arrived at her house - the smell of the mountain air and the feel of it on my skin, the gently clanking sheep bells in the distance.

It was 2.30 in the morning and it was Natacha's 30th birthday.

The whole place was twinkling with the flickering flames of candles that led us up the path all the way to the house and fringed the whole veranda. The roof beams were festooned with flags, the upright posts garlanded by strings of organic apples. On the table there was a huge box of fresh organic vegetable plants

- lettuce, cabbage, onion and carrot - and a large card with a photo of Natacha.

Natacha could hardly believe her eyes. Sabina, her friend, had secretly arranged to set all this up while she was out of the house when she was meeting me in Palma. Natacha, for her part, was quite overwhelmed by the trouble that her lovely kind, caring and loving friend had taken to make it a special day.

When we eventually got to bed at about 3.00 a.m. we both had a good night's sleep. In the morning we feasted on a delicious, healthy breakfast of organic toast, topped with avocado, home grown tomatoes and some bean sprouts that I had brought over.

The day was to hold more delightful surprises. Natacha's parents, Hélène and Gerard, had been able to book a table for lunch at a fabulous restaurant, Micelli, in Silva. It's an old finca in the centre of the village and it is so popular that you have to book three weeks in advance. Natacha's grandfather was also with us. From our table we could see an old windmill in front of the restaurant and behind it stretched magnificent views across the wide valley to the mountains in the distance. The food was exquisite and consisted of many small dishes, including vegan and vegetarian ones for Natacha and me. I felt so blessed to be part of this beautiful family.

We spent the afternoon processing Natacha's dried figs. There were quite a few of us and we were each allocated a job, learning what to do as we worked.

A friend of Natacha's was letting her use the oven to dry the figs so we had to collect the washed jars and the figs and take them across to her friend's house.

Natacha began by bringing a huge pan of water to the boil, with a fig leaf and some fennel seed heads and stalks in the water. When the water was boiling, she dunked a basket of figs into it for 30 seconds three times in succession in order to kill any insects that might be in the fruits. The figs were then left to drain for a while and, when most of the water had drained away, they were put into the oven at 110° for 25 minutes. They were then laid out on a cloth to cool and, once cooled, they were packed down tightly in the jars between layers of carob leaves and fennel stalks. The packing down was done with a wooden dibber used for squashing garlic, and the jars were filled right to the very top. Finally, after a short time with their lids open, the jars were tightly closed.

After three hours of hard work we had processed 50 kilos of figs. There were three of us doing it. The previous year Natacha had done it all on her own.

Her friend Willow treated us all to freshly picked

bunches of grapes when we were finished.

Since Natacha now had a job working in an organic restaurant she was out during the day. I stayed at home while she was at work thoroughly enjoying the peace and tranquillity of the place. It was late by the time she got home, and then we had to go and say goodbye to her parents, who were returning to Ibiza.

After that we went over to her farm. I was very excited to see what changes she had made since the year before.

There were two big changes. One was that, during the winter she had planted several more fig trees, in a circle. The other was that she had bought some donkeys - a male and a female. Only, when she had gone to the farm to check on them a few days after she had got them, she'd found that she had three donkeys! Imagine her surprise! Unbeknown to Natacha, the female had been pregnant and had now produced a baby donkey. Apparently donkeys have a lot of babies! So now the baby was six weeks old and so cute.

The donkeys serve two purposes - they clear the land of weeds and at the same time, of course, they manure the land. But three donkeys need a lot of looking after, and they have to be watched in case they get up to any mischief. Natacha told me how, even though the big donkeys were tied up so that they wouldn't eat the trees, they did get away from time to time. On one occasion, when they had managed to break free, they had eaten Natacha's almond grafts. It would have set the almond growth back a lot and was a great shame. The trees had borne a lot of fruit and it was doubtful that they would ever fully recover.

One day while I was staying with her we had to wait at the farm for the lorry to deliver water. We decided to climb up the mountain while we were waiting and we sat on a rock on the top, overlooking the farm and enjoying our picnic. Suddenly Natacha noticed that the female donkey had become untethered. This was worrying because apparently the male could attack and kill both mother and baby during the first few months after the birth. Natacha had been making sure that they were kept well apart and couldn't see each other. We were a long way up and there was no way we could get down in a hurry to avert disaster. Natacha tried to phone some people below who were working close by, but they didn't answer, so we packed up quickly and sped down the mountain. When we reached the bottom, though, we found that the mother and baby had made their way to the house. A young man, seeing them wandering loose, had tied them up safe and sound.

Her house, in its prime location with fabulous views of the mountains and the valley, was also coming on in leaps and bounds now. Natacha's dream was to live a life close to nature, in harmony with nature, in a yurt or straw bale house. Her father, though, was insisting that she have a modern house with all mod cons and simply could not understand her vision - to have people living close to nature helping her to bring into practice the permaculture principles that she so passionately believed in. I understood her completely. It's magical seeing everything unfold in the natural world.

SOLLER

'The 24th September has dawned. I donned my rucksack and provisions and caught the bus from Caimari to Lluc Monastery. The driver told me to sit down and asked the little boy sitting next to him to give me a ticket, but didn't take the money until I got off the bus. Everything is very laid back. Lovely to see! The driver talked animatedly to the boys while he drove around the many mountain bends. There was a big group of children with musical instruments, accompanied by their teacher, also on their way to Lluc to play and sing in the monastery in the choir that goes back centuries.'

I stayed at the Monastery in Lluc for one night before

catching the bus for Soller the next day. After I had been waiting for a very long time for the bus someone in the restaurant told me that it had been cancelled - just like that! Then I found out that there was going to be a cycle race through the mountains that day. The restaurant ordered a taxi for me - luckily I had enough money to pay for one. But when I told the driver where I was going, to a Bed and Breakfast called Eco Cirer, he didn't recognise the address. It was a new Bed and Breakfast. I tried to phone them but couldn't get in touch with them because they didn't pick up my calls. I began to get anxious about finding it.

The drive through the mountains was magnificent but, as all my attempts to call for directions were unsuccessful, my anxiety continued to mount as we drew closer to Soller. Then luckily, when we were nearly there, they phoned me back. The taxi driver dropped me off at the bus station in the village and someone from the Bed and Breakfast came to pick me up.

It had been quite a stressful journey, so I was delighted by the oasis of peace and tranquillity that met my eyes when Barbara, the owner, opened the gate onto a beautiful cobbled courtyard. There were pots filled with plants everywhere. A Nispero (medlar) tree in the corner provided summer shade. Another huge tree at the end of the garden was festooned by a climbing Bignonia that flamboyantly spilled fronds of pink tubular flowers all over it. There was an entrance at the back that fronted the railway line, where there was the occasional sound of a train or whistle as it left Soller for Palma. But despite that I felt that this was going to be the perfect place to unwind.

'I have a room to myself, apart from the house. There are lovely little touches everywhere. A deep maroon rose with some greenery on the bedside table on one side, a lily on the other. Outside the room, on a shelf displaying adverts for places to eat and a guest book, there is another yellow rose in a vase. The mattress is a natural one just like the one I have at home. The bathroom has a spacious shower and bottles of shampoo and shower gel. There's a message on each of the bottles "Stop the water while using me!" Such a good idea to save water.'

'Much attention is given to recycling. Three stacked boxes form a table. A sack is used as a rug. Outside pallets are hung on the wall for plants. Unusual abstract paintings adorn the walls. My room is called Chamomile, I would like to come back to the same room if I come again.'

'We eat our vegetarian or vegan breakfast at small individual tables outside in the courtyard, surrounded

by plants. There is a vase of fresh flowers to greet you. The breakfasts are quite different to any I have had before. Everything is organic. Much of it is grown on their own land. There are strings of tomatoes hung up in the house for winter use. At present they have only renovated two rooms. They have another five rooms to do.'

The village of Soller is nestled in the mountains. There's a cross at the top of one of the mountains, with a footpath leading up to it. I decided, one day, to walk up there. After losing my way twice I ended up going through a beautiful garden. There was an outside kitchen and it looked as though people had barbecues there. At the end of it there was another gate leading out to a path, so I went through and followed the path again, until I reached a locked gate. I could see the cross, but I couldn't get to it, so I made my way back to the garden.

I decided to sit and read my book, *Cave in the Snow* by Vicki Mackenzie - a very interesting book about a woman who became a nun and lived alone in a cave high in the Himalayas for twelve years. After a while two other women came through the garden. I discovered that they had also got lost and they decided to go back down again. I carried on reading. It was a lovely, enjoyable interlude. I was feeling lucky to have stumbled upon this idyllic place looking over mountains to the sea in the distance on a lovely sunny day. Then a young woman came along and told me I was in a private garden!

When I got back to the B & B I asked Barbara about the locked gate at the top. She told me that it had probably been closed to stop people taking picnics there because they always left rubbish and dog mess lying around. She is very sad about it and so was I.

One day, during my four-day stay at Soller, I decided to take a bus to Deia. I missed one bus because someone had given me wrong information, so I had an hour to wait until the next one.

The bus took us through spectacular scenery to high in the mountains. I walked the cobbled streets around the village and up to the cemetery, feeling that I had gone back in time to a past era. At the top of the mountain there was a magnificent view across the mountains and valleys – my soul food. Then I found a lovely restaurant where I enjoyed a fresh fish lunch surrounded by mountains and basking in the sunshine.

Not many buses run between those mountain villages. After my experience in the morning, I made sure to get to the stop 45 minutes before it was due. I waited and waited, and then waited some more. The bus didn't

come. The waiting crowd grew larger by the minute.
The new people were starting to congregate in front of
those of us who had been waiting a long time.

And of course, when a bus did eventually arrive it
already had many people on it. I was almost aboard
when the driver announced that it was full, and left the
rest of us standing by the roadside. By now I had been
waiting for two hours! Now there was a scramble of
people trying to get taxis, so that was a no-go. I
decided to try and get a lift from someone in the car
park.

I asked one man who was taking two ladies but he said
he had no room. The next person I went to ask didn't
have room either. By now it was getting late and I was
quite fed up. I simply stood there in the middle of the
car park, put my hands together in front of my heart,
and asked my angels, "Please, please can you get me a
lift as I am fed up and tired now." Out of the blue, I
heard a call from the first man I had approached,
saying he would take me after all.

"Thank you angels!"

They are there with you and me all the time. You just
need to ask.

On another day I went to visit the local botanic garden.

I am always nurtured and feel in my element being with plants. The gardens were much better than I had expected them to be and, of course, I had to buy two cactus plants, didn't I! I hadn't realised that you can root cacti from their leaves, so I gave Natacha some leaves to propagate herself.

When it was time to leave Soller a French man who was staying at the B & B offered to take me to the bus station. I took the bus back to Lluc and from there I got a taxi back to Natacha's, where I waited until she got back from work. Then we went to Ginebro restaurant in Inca for our last meal together.

Early next morning she drove me back to Palma to catch the boat back to Ibiza before she headed on to work. I boarded the ferry back home armed with a mass of various plants, cuttings, and cacti. As we sailed out of Palma I saw a spaceship lit up from behind by the sun. What a send off!

A rainbow greeted me as my welcome back to Ibiza when we arrived back. How magnificent is that!

chapter thirty five
Satish Kumar

Satish Kumar is a man after my own heart. A former monk and long-term peace activist, his influence has spread around the world. His book, *No Destination,* is the fascinating account of his two-and-a-half-year-long peace walk from Delhi to New York, done without any money.

I have his permission to quote this excerpt from it.

"At the ecological level, humanity has been at war with nature. Our desire to conquer nature has led to destruction of wilderness, reduction of biodiversity, production of poisonous chemicals, construction of megacities, mega-dams, mega-industries and mega-corporations. This has resulted in polluted seas and rivers, polluted air, depleted foods, and eroded land. Our cruelty to animals, our disregard for traditional tribal cultures and their rights, our relentless drive to extract oil and other minerals without limit are all part of the same story."

'He writes about being peaceful in our everyday lives. Now as I write in early November 2016 tribes are uniting to save their land and water at Standing Rock reservation Dakota. They are peacefully protesting and praying. This has brought many Native American tribes together. This is something that is unprecedented.

The police have so far shot two of their horses, sprayed indigenous people with pepper spray in their eyes, used rubber bullets and sprayed water at the people in cold temperatures. Unbelievable what people can do to each other just for monetary gain, to lay a pipeline for moving oil which if leaked would destroy thousands of peoples' drinking water like it has done with other leaks. So many people are being galvanised to take part in the demonstration, even the war veterans are due to join them on December 4th.'

chapter thirty six

Walking the Camino – Inner Shifts

In April 2017 I spent five weeks walking the Camino de Compostela from León to Santiago.

How this came about and what I experienced during my pilgrimage are chronicled in a separate book, *My Camino at 81 – It's Never Too Late,* that I wrote on my return to Ibiza.

After I got back from the Camino I had a sense that many things were going to happen, and so they did. I began to feel as though everything was unfolding to set me onto a new path at high speed and it felt like the beginning of a new chapter in my life.

Curiously, what began the whole process was a visit to a shaman, Diane Whitehorse Spirit. While I had been on the Camino I had begun to suffer from a constant putrid smell in my nose, and it had not gone away, even after I got back to Ibiza. Apparently a persistent negative entity, a brutal old mediaeval monk had attached itself to me while I was on the Camino. I had gone to see if Diane could clear it for me. What followed was astonishing.

The first thing she told me was that my husband was still hooked into me. I was flabbergasted. I did not think that this could be the case once someone had passed over. She also said that my husband had put a block in my throat, because he had always talked for me. When I asked her if he had known he was doing this, she answered that he may have been doing it unconsciously. She pulled him out energetically and afterwards I wrote, *'I feel so, so good now. He had probably been stopping me from meeting someone else.'*

She went on to tell me that my husband had put a wedge between my eldest daughter, who was confused, and myself, she said. My daughter had not talked to me since I had published my first book in 2012 because I had written about her father. Truth is, I had always been piggy-in-the-middle between my husband and her and I felt that she had laid all her guilt on to me, as she had never got on with him.

My view on what I had written was that I couldn't write an autobiography and leave the main part out. I had told all my children that it was their choice whether or not they read the book. The other two did not read it, so they don't know anything about me. For a long time I carried around a burden of guilt about my daughter's behaviour towards me. It hurt me deeply and it affected my feelings towards her. Knowing what I know now, I look at things in a totally different perspective.

'I have not fallen out with my daughter, and never will. It is her problem. I have been working on myself to clear any traumas with her, which is helping enormously.'

I cannot imagine falling out with my Mum, whatever she might have done, even if I did not like it. Soon, though I didn't know it at the time, my mother's energy would be with me again.

I write about this in the hope that it will help people who are in similar family situations. As Eckhart Tolle puts it, "We play games with our mind. We need to be in stillness, no past, no future. Just be." Dwelling on things instead of letting go of what we cannot change just holds us back.

On a positive note, the best present I received on the Camino was a text from my son, which said, "Well Done!" He never texts or phones me normally, so it was a big surprise. I found out later that he had seen a documentary about the Camino that made him realise just what I had done. His view was that it was a coincidence that he had seen the documentary. I know different! He had watched the same documentary that had jogged my memory to walk the Camino in the first place!

At the end of June I went to a tarot reader who told me that I would clear a lot of karma before three moons had passed.

'Have been working on myself ever since. Have cleared so much and it's nearly the third full moon'

TRIBAL GATHERING

In July I joined an Aniwa Tribal Gathering on Ibiza. I felt so blessed to live on an island where people come from all over the world for events like this.

It was a 4-day long gathering bringing indigenous elders, leaders, and master shamans together with western teachers and musicians for a culture exchange and unified prayer. The intention was to unite nations through the sharing of their teachings, their art, their music, and their culture; and to unify in prayer for the preservation of indigenous cultures and the protection of our mother Earth – to create one universal tribe.

Nothing quite went to plan, as aptly described by Nicholas, a young Australian who left the comfort zone of his steady nine-to-five job to find his spiritual truth travelling the world. I come in contact with so many young people like him. Nicholas made a video about the event and commented,

"After a wobbly start the gathering manifested into such full power of indigenous Elder knowledge and a medicine melting pot.

We have to let go of expectations (there is always a greater plan unfolding behind the scenes.) Such an interesting experience that unfolded in the last few days, where literally the whole programme collapsed. Everything that was meant to unfold, fell back into the void of nothingness. Something completely new and miraculous emerged, and so sometimes, what we expect to happen in life does not happen."

Everyone was really tested and asked to really surrender all expectations, so something new could emerge. There are twenty tribes from the Maoris in New Zealand, Dogons from Africa; we have Elders from North, Central, and South America who came to represent the indigenous wisdom. Such a beautiful gift to be in their presence.

Police came on the first day and tried to shut the event down. It did not meet the regulations and they did not get permission. The Tribes said this happens all the time. Everybody breathed and prayed. We all had to be with it. There is a lot of love, very challenging in a beautiful way. We have to let go. Like going down a river where we don't know where we are going and have to trust the process of the unknown. So many changes, so many upsets, so many detours. Keep breathing, keep laughing, keep having fun on the way, as we surrender. As the light meets the dark, dark meets the light. We have to go deep in ourselves, into a deeper space of unity.

I went to a breath workshop while I was at the Gathering. This time I had a profound experience the like of which I had not had during the Breath Retreat that I had been on previously. As the workshop was coming to an end the leader, Rebecca Dennis, told us to bring in the light. Suddenly I felt as though there was a skullcap round the top of my head, and I had the sensation twice. I started to cry, could not stop, and wanted to carry on but the workshop was over. All the same I felt that I had had an amazing experience and cleared a lot of deep-rooted karma. I wasn't the only one who had a profound experience that day - there was one girl who could not talk for crying, and another who went out of her body.

Later that day, as I was just going into the tunnel to look at indigenous paintings, there was a woman at the entrance clearing auras.

As the old monk's spirit was still plaguing me, I asked her if she cleared spirits. Telling me that she had been guided there, she took me to a place to work on me, but was then channelled that the place was too noisy. Her name was Vicki Sinclair. She came from Ireland and she said she could come to my house on Tuesday. I felt it was a bit soon after my other clearing, so she eventually came on the Thursday.

She cleared a lot of inner child stuff that I had been holding onto.

During my session with her I remembered how jealous I had been of my sister when we were children. I remembered that I'd had to have surgery at the age of three after swallowing a copper weight. I had also suffered the trauma of being a very young child during the Second World War. Vicki told me that all of these experiences would have been pushed down into my subconscious because I would have not wanted to think about them.

I just had the one clearing with her and it did shift

some stuff. After that and the Breath Week work I did feel considerably better.

'I feel so great now without all these burdens.'

THE RIGHTNESS OF WHEN THINGS DON'T GO TO PLAN

It is pretty incredible how we are shown the way.

I wanted to do a lot of clearing during those summer months and had booked another young Irish woman to come to my house to do some more of the deep work. On the day that she was due to come I got a text message from her telling me that she'd had to go to Dublin urgently. I didn't see the message until it was time for the appointment.

I made another appointment with her, for three weeks later, and on the due morning messaged her on Facebook to ask her if she knew where to come. When I went to see if she had responded, I found that my Facebook was down. This was really weird. I texted a friend to see if hers was also down, but hers was working perfectly normally.

So I sat in the garden with my phone, waiting for the young woman to call me. Whenever anyone was coming to visit me for the first time I would go to the gate to meet him or her to show the way to my tucked away little casita. No call came. I went back indoors only to find that now my Facebook was up again.

Later, when we finally did make contact with one another, she was very irate. She told me that she'd been sitting outside the gate for 20 minutes and had tried to call, but hadn't been able to get through.

I firmly believe that I was not meant to have her to work with me.

I try to listen to my inner self and am usually guided as to what I should do.

chapter thirty seven

Inner Child Healing

The following Saturday I decided to do a liquid detox.

Curiously, at my next yoga class we did a yoga detox, using some very powerful asanas and breathing exercises. The effects were so profound that I fell asleep at the end of it and afterwards couldn't remember what exercises I had done. Getting into the car to leave, I felt very weird and asked my angels to look after me on the way home. On the way I stopped at the farm shop at Can Muson to buy some organic fruit and vegetables. I tried to ground myself again with a cup of coffee and a juice, but the sense of disorientation persisted. When I got home I slept deeply for two hours.

When I told Ria later about it all she explained that I

was integrating a lot of stuff. She also said that I was clearly not meant to have worked with the woman that I had not succeeded in meeting up with.

By the end of August I was feeling the need for some more breath work to clear more of my inner child. I knew I had a lot of clearing to do with my mother and my father. I found a photo of Aloka on the internet and felt very drawn to her. I had met her at Solara's once and now I felt that she was the person to work with.

My father came through. Aloka asked me to tell him how I felt as a child. I said, "I did not feel loved. I was never cuddled. My Dad told my mother not to cuddle me as it would spoil me." I cried a lot and cleared a lot during the session. Finally I forgave him and hugged him in a child-like way. It was very powerful. He said he was pleased that I was healing.

Then my mother came through. I told her how my sister and I had felt very frightened when she went upstairs in the dark and hid from us. We thought she had left us. I also told her, "I did not get any cuddles." In the end we forgave each other with love and hugged each other. She sent me pink roses, straight to my heart. Again it was all so very powerful.

'I feel I have cleared so much more now, slowly peeling back the layers of the onion. I now have a photo of her

90th birthday on my altar.'

Afterwards I started having more pleasant memories of my childhood. I remembered how much I enjoyed eating porridge from a shallow willow pattern bowl. As I was eating I was revealing more of the poem that my mother would tell us about the pictures,

"Two birds above go flying high,

A little ship a sailing by,

Two men on a bridge, if not four,

A weeping willow hanging o'er.

A giant's castle there it stands

As if it were the law of lands.

A tree above with apples on,

A fence below to end the song."

Then memories came back of another delightful little poem that my mother used to recite to us. I think you will enjoy it.

Little Flo's Letter

Anonymous

"A sweet little baby brother has come to live with Flo. She wanted him brought to the table so he could eat and grow.

'You must wait awhile,' said Grandma-ma in answer to her plea,

'for the poor little thing that has no teeth, can't eat like you and me.'

'Why hasn't he got teeth Grandma-ma?' asked Flo in great surprise.

'Oh isn't it funny - no teeth but nose and eyes.'

That afternoon to a corner with paper, pen and ink,

Went Flo saying, 'don't talk to me you'll disturb my fink.

I'm writing a letter, Grandma-ma, and its got to go tonight,

And because it is very important, I want to get it right.'

At last the letter was finished,

a wonderful thing to see directed to God in heaven.

'Please read it over to me,' asked little Flo to her Grandma,

'To see if it is right you know.'

And here is the letter written to God by little Flo.

'Dear God the baby you sent us is very nice and sweet,

but because you forgot his toothies, the poor little thing can't eat.

That is why I am writing this letter, on purpose to let you know,

Please come and finish our baby, that's all....from little Flo.'"

chapter thirty eight

My Vision for the Planet

I meditated all summer on how I would like to see this beautiful planet that is our habitat.

First of all, what a difference it would make if there were no plastic or drinks tins and nothing were wrapped in plastic. I saw something on the internet about a young woman who opened a shop in England run along these lines, where people would take along jars to be filled in the shop. It is possible and my hope is that this manifests in more shops.

Thinking about children, I would like there to be no red tape in schools so that teachers wouldn't have to waste so much time on paperwork. Yoga and meditation would be part of the curriculum and the schools would have creative things for children to do.

They would have more art and music. They would learn to do laundry and cooking. I cooked at school and would delight in taking something that I had cooked home to my mother.

I would teach them how to grow vegetables and flowers and how to interact with nature, learning about birds, butterflies, dragonflies, insects. I would provide a pond so that children could learn more about nature and pond life. My son used to spend hours watching the fish and other insects in our pond then, when we walked along the rivers in Devon, he could always see the fish that I had difficulty in seeing.

I would like to see pristine seas with turtles coming back to eat the jellyfish, keeping nature in balance, and dolphins freely swimming in the sea, not eating and being killed by the rubbish we throw into it. They are very intelligent animals and can teach us a great deal.

There would be forests with diverse varieties of trees. There is so much that we do not know about trees and how they keep nature in balance. They can house hundreds of different kinds of insects that feed the birds. Grown along the coast they provide us with rain. Mushrooms growing under the trees that feed everything around them.

My vision is of a planet where there is no engineering

of the weather and an abundance of food organically grown; no GMOs.

It's a planet with no passports, where we can travel freely to any country, where people from all over the world integrate with each other. There are no taxes, no controls on people, just people working together to create a new world, living with nature as the tribes have always done. No fear. Everybody helping each other in love, compassion and gratitude.

Let's work together to achieve a magical planet where we live in peace.

As I thought about these things I added, *'I am looking forward to a time when we can be much more self-sufficient on this island, therefore cutting down on pollution.'*

'I remember when there were no package holidays with flights, when there was one company just starting up that did package holidays by boat and train. We used to go abroad with our car and camp. We visited many countries this way. The holiday companies have escalated since that time, polluting the atmosphere. We need to get back to living more in tune and balance with nature.'

chapter thirty nine

A Tale of Redemption

In October 2017 a friend of mine, Angie, suggested that I should meet a young man that she knew. We had something in common – the Camino. Govinda had just returned from walking his pilgrimage.

We met for lunch at La Paloma, a restaurant in the countryside in San Lorenç where you can enjoy organic food sitting under the orange trees. I had felt quite pleased with myself, having walked the Camino at the age of 81. Now I was to be truly impressed when Govinda told me about the lady who had walked the whole Camino - 800 kilometres – at the age of 93! He also told me that she practised yoga everyday. What an amazing lady!

Then he told me his own story.

GOVINDA'S STORY

'It all **began in the European Summer of 2006. It's a** story I could not make up, even if I plucked it from the depths of my wildest imagination.

I had just successfully obtained a Maltese passport through the divine blood of my mother Marie Morris. You see, she was born in Malta before migrating to Australia with her family.

My mum, sadly, had life taken from her at the tender age of 35, in 1982. She left behind those who loved her most - her two young sons. This Maltese passport, one of the many legacies my beautiful Mum left me was, in my mind, my "ticket to freedom." It afforded me, a young Australian man, the opportunity to live and work anywhere in Europe that my heart called me to go.

Ibiza had been a place that I had dreamed of visiting for many years. In my mind, I saw it as a place of hedonism and wild abandon, and of freedom. My love for house music and dancing was unparalleled, so it seemed to me like paradise. I had always promised myself that I would go and visit the island, maybe even experience working a summer season there once I secured the Maltese passport.

It was destined to be all that I dreamed it was, and so much more. More than I could possibly have foreseen.

I was living in Sydney. It was summer 2006. The time was now, and I started to make plans to work in Ibiza for that coming European summer. Five crazy months of living on an island that is home to some of the best and most amazing clubs in the world! "Yeah...!" I thought, "That's for me!" An endless party, an endless summer – these thoughts were all the coaxing that I needed to pack up my life in Sydney and hit the White Island.

I arrived in Ibiza that May with a suitcase full of summer clothes, a bank account full of money, and a head full of dreams of making it big on the White Island. To say I was excited would be a massive understatement. My heart and soul knew that this experience would be one of the most incredible experiences of my life to date.

With my EU passport firmly in hand and a heart fit to explode, I worked on making the most of the contacts I had made over the past ten years, working in clubs and entertainment. I was ready to rock and roll! Arriving on the White Island was magical. I booked myself into a hotel in Figuretas for the first week, just to get my bearings and check out what the island had to offer.

I was very fortunate in many ways to have the help of my friends David Morales and Barbara Tucker. They had both been very well known performers on the island for many years. Through Barbara I got a job as a PR person for her party, *In Bed with Space*, one of the biggest parties on the island that started in the wee A.M. hours at that infamous club, Space.

The job entailed roaming the beaches in and around Ibiza, giving out wristbands for cheaper entry. It was a great opportunity not only to connect with extraordinary people from all over the world, but also to promote what I thought was a cool party.

Day after day I got out there and worked hard promoting this party on the hot white sands of Ibiza in the blazing heat of summer. The money wasn't great. You worked on a commission based structure. The more wristbands you gave out that were ultimately handed in on the day of the party, the more money you would make.

This job though, raised other opportunities - opportunities that would be both rewarding and exceptionally destructive, as I would eventually find out.

Party people from all over the world come to lose themselves in the hedonistic world of Ibiza. I was meeting them daily, and over and over again this question would come up, "Can you help us out with any drugs?"

Let's get one thing straight I loved my drugs, and I loved to party! When I say I loved my drugs, I mean recreational drugs, "party drugs" like ecstasy, MDMA, special K (a horse tranquilliser) and a joint occasionally. Would I say I was an addict?? Hmmm that was questionable to be completely honest. Did I take these drugs every day?? NO. When I partied YES.

I remember the first time I went out in Ibiza. I was a guest of Dailey Morales at his weekly night at Pacha. I was like a kid in a candy shop. I had my on best party outfit, a pocket full of uppers *and* was on David's guest list. What more could I want? I had arrived. Or so I thought then...

The night was beyond magical. I danced for hours and got high and let it all go!! I had a taste for the nightlife in Ibiza, the wild heat of a place with the sole purpose of focusing on pleasure. It was like something running through my veins and actually connecting to my heart.

I continued working in PR, meeting more and more people and kind of enjoying my time doing it. That is, apart from the crap money. It seemed like no matter how many people I met, and handed out those coveted wristbands, I was just barely making ends meet. Ibiza, as fun as it is, is a place where it's hard to have fun, if you don't have a LOT of cash. Everything, and I mean everything, had a price.

The summer was well under way and the energy of the island was high! I was grateful to be living there, living the dream I'd had for so many years. I was vibrating. It was all I had hoped for...but it was about to be so much more...

Everything was to change in a moment that I will never forget. It would set me on a path that would change my life in a way that was unfathomable at that time. I remember the day so clearly, that day when a "friend," (well some one that I had just met that summer) said to me, "You should consider selling some drugs on the side, seeing you're out there in the beaches and promoting this party. Why not?" Why not indeed!

He gave me the figures and costing of the product. In an instant I worked out that I could make a lot of money very quickly. Nothing is more attractive in Ibiza, than a way to make quick money to allow you to live the high life that is all around you. Everywhere. The temptation was irresistible.

Not to say that I didn't give this more than a moment's thought. I did. I thought this over and over and over, constantly. I spoke to a few other friends about it, confiding in them what I was thinking of doing. They too were selling. It seemed to be an accepted way of life in Ibiza.

So, I set my course, and said, " YES."

I met him in a safe place to arrange the exchange of money for drugs. I was nervous, but I was also excited - my adrenaline was flowing. I bought 50 ecstasy pills at €3 each. I could sell them for €10 each, so the mark-up was pretty good. Starting with this amount was manageable without too much of a risk of losing the money.

I was relatively new to this, I was in a country that was not my own, and I was nervous, but I wasn't stupid. I wouldn't sell on the beach like all those other rookies. I resolved to give out my number to people asking for party treats. That way I could meet them in the safety of their hotel or villa. It gave me some protection from consequences that I preferred not think about. If I am to be completely honest, I thought I was invincible. The thought of getting caught, or even what I was doing was completely wrong and unlawful never even crossed my mind. The way I looked at it was, I'm helping people have fun. Simple as that!!!

I remember meeting my first client at a hotel in Figuretas. I had 50 ecstasy pills, 5 grams of coke (that I was selling for a friend), and 5 grams of special K. I remember the buzz I was feeling as I left the villa, having just offloaded the entire stash of drugs to those tourists that just arrived in Ibiza for their summer holidays.

When I returned to my home in Figuretas I eagerly counted all the money I had made. I had a profit of something around the figure of €500! This was a far cry from the tiny amount I could make slaving away as a PR person on the beach. Right there something ignited in me and I thought, "If I can do this once, surely, I can push the boundaries and do it again."

So, I ordered more supplies - double the amount this time. I do remember walking down the Paseo in Figuretas after picking them up feeling a little nervous about the sheer quantity of drugs that I was carrying on my person. But, I was invincible, and of course, this time, I made it home safely.

That next week, perhaps from the relief of getting away with this new life I was living, I proceeded to go out and get completely smashed. I hit Bora Bora, on Playa de Bossa, every afternoon, and even went to DC10, where I remember getting so trashed that I could hardly walk.

That week of partying took its toll on my health. I had been completely out of control. I was full of toxins and illegal substances. It was only to be expected that I would eventually become very unwell. The come down lasted a whole week. I had such a bad head cold and I was taking a large

amount of cold and flu medication. That week I stayed clean from taking any recreational drugs whatsoever.

It was early Sunday morning, 15th September 2006. The phone buzzed with a text message. A client was asking for a large amount of party treats. I didn't think twice. I set up the meet-up time and location, and off I went, dressed in shorts, a T-shirt and flip-flops. Still not completely well from my come down and head cold, I was sluggish and not my usual self. In a word, I was not as sharp as I normally would have been.

My tiny Adidas vintage bag contained 120 ecstasy pills, 5 grams of coke, 5 grams of special K and a small block of hash. I headed off to Playa de Bossa. Just then a friend offered to drive me there. I accepted. I never gave it a moment's pause for thought. Of course my friend would help me out. Why would there be anything unusual about that? Well.... the answer to this question was one that would alter the course of my existence.

As we drive down the strip of Bossa, he decides, unexpectedly, to turn into the Space car park. Within seconds five or six Guardia Civil officers surround the car. My heart practically stops. I go deaf. From here on in everything goes into slow motion. I am the fly in the spider's web. I have been caught, and any movement is futile. I know my luck has run out. There is literally nothing I can do but surrender.

As I open my door I look down at my Adidas bag and realise there is nothing I can do with the bag.

The lady officer takes my bag and opens it...BOOOM!!

Handcuffs go straight on, Snap snap, and I'm captured right before my very eyes.

I'm numb with fear, terrified of the unknown, and truly scared for my life. They place me in the police car and off we drive. My heart is hammering, banging in my ears. It's the only thing I can hear. And my mind - my mind is whirring at warp speed.

The first stop is the Guardia Civil headquarters at the airport. I'm taken into a room where I'm questioned by the authorities, mostly in Spanish. I am lost. I don't understand anything that is being said. I'm made to wait until an interpreter who speaks English arrives.

"What are you doing with all these drugs" the interpreter demands. I reply, "They are for the closing parties for myself and my friends." It's all I can think of. I have seen enough TV shows, and have enough of a sense of self-preservation to know that subterfuge is probably a "good" starting point.

He's not having a bar of my story whatsoever. It doesn't help that the drugs are all packaged individually. That immediately gives it away that they are, indeed, for distribution.

"You are in serious trouble with this number of drugs."

At this point the seriousness of my situation hits me like a freight train. Again I deny that they are for sale and stick to my story that they are, indeed, for personal use.

I am drugs tested. The endless interrogations continue. I am absolutely terrified. I have no idea what to do. I am alone and scared, and someone that I trusted sold me out. I pray for the ground to swallow me up and for me to just disappear from this hell.

As it was a Sunday the courts were closed, and I could not appear to make a case for bail. So I was taken to a holding cell somewhere in San Antonio. I remember walking into that cold filthy cell praying to God that I would be protected, begging him for salvation, begging just to live, even if it was just for right now.

That night was like being in hell. I was still recovering from my sickness. I was cold. All I had was a dirty blanket and piece of cardboard to sleep on. All night different people were brought into the holding cell. Who knew who these people were, what they had done, or what they would want to do to me? It was a purely terrifying experience that left me feeling raw, vulnerable and fearing for my life. I have never felt so incredibly afraid.

The next morning, still handcuffed, I was transported to the courts in Ibiza town where I was again interrogated for hours.

"We are giving you one more chance to tell us the truth about the drugs." Stoically, I continued to stick to my story!

I was seated in front of a few official court authorities. The next moment was a blur and all I remember was seeing a document with the word PRISON written large across the top of it. My heart sank to the lowest point imaginable. Is this really happening? Is this just a bad nightmare that I will awake from in the morning? NO..... This was my reality!! I was faced with the situation that I was going to prison. Me, this fun-loving, uplifting, funny and positive person! Luck had run out right before my very eyes.

I broke down in deep emotion, terrified that my life was over, that I had danced with the devil one too many times, and that taking shortcuts in life would be my downfall.

I prayed to God and begged my mum in heaven to protect me and give me courage even just to get through the next second of this complete disaster that I had got myself into.

As the police van pulled into the prison, located only 10 minutes out of Ibiza town, I knew my beautiful wings had really been clipped. My ability to soar high in the sky would be a dream of days gone past.

I was taken to my own tiny, concrete cell that measured just 3 m x 4 m and had three bunk beds along one side. It had its own toilet and a small wash sink, and it was filthy. A small window overlooked an outdoor square.

I asked the officer for a pen and paper. I knew I needed to write, to share my emotions and what I was experiencing right now, sitting alone in this cell. I wrote and wrote and wrote, pouring out exactly what I was feeling. I wrote about my fears, my dreams, and my vision of my life. It helped to calm me and bring me into my heart's space, exactly where I needed to be.

It was the end of the summer. The prison was full of people who had been incarcerated for crimes committed on Ibiza. So for almost a whole week I was in my own cell.

Then, one morning I was taken out of my cell to meet a lawyer called Ricardo, whom my brother had found through a friend of his. Ricardo was Spanish, middle-aged, quite friendly and spoke English.

It was time for me to be completely honest with him. I explained that I had, indeed, intended to sell the drugs. At that point he explained that the public prosecutor was giving me three years in prison for this crime. Three years??? I was beyond shocked. Just one week being locked up, my freedom taken from me, was private hell.

Ricardo's take on this was to plead that I was an addict, and that I wasn't mentally well. The strike in pleading our case that I was an addict was the fact that when I was originally arrested the drugs tests were negative.

Now I was transferred into the main area of the prison. Fear set in at the thought that I would be surrounded by other inmates, other men. Brutal men. This absolutely terrified me. Walking into that area that morning is a memory that that will remain etched into my mind forever. I took a deep breath and prayed to God to keep me safe. I mean, a gay man who basically stood out was not a good position to be in, especially in this situation.

I kept to myself.

A lovely English chap came up to me and started chatting. I was so relieved, so grateful and so thankful for this small act of kindness. "What're you in for?" he asked. I couldn't believe that I was actually hearing myself utter these words: "Drugs." Turned out he had been involved in a fight outside a club, and thrown into jail for it.

The minutes turned to hours, the hours to days, the days to weeks. Before you knew it I had been inside for a month.

Meanwhile Ricardo was doing everything to get the three-year sentence converted to release on bail, to attend rehab. As expected, it wasn't so easy to gain this option.

To keep myself sane while was incarcerated I wrote lots of letters. I wrote to family and friends. They wrote back. These letters would become my lifeline to the outside world, a world that I had taken for granted before. As I faced the reality that, for now I was locked up and just a number and a case waiting to be heard, those letters let me have hope, just a little, but enough for now.

In no time, I had letters coming to me from all over the world, from friends, family and people that I had never even met. I remember receiving a letter from my great uncle Moz. Moz had been a prisoner of war in Asia for over four years back in the 1970's. That letter gave me the courage, the strength and the power to put one foot in front of another. To this day, I have kept all these letters. They are a big part of the book that I am in the process of writing about my experiences.

Then, one afternoon Ricardo brought news that there was some kind of light at the end of tunnel. For the first time in a long time, I allowed myself to smile. The public prosecutor was at least *considering* the exchange of the three years for rehab. Now I clung so tightly to this only hope as a way out of that prison, and prayed dearly for this outcome.

I did have another lifeline during those months spent behind bars. I called her my Guardian Angel. She was my case manager, Angela, a divine English lady who would come into the prison to look after all the western inmates. We connected, and I knew I had someone in her who cared and wanted me to be free. She gave me light when there was none.

I am so grateful that she is in my life and keep in contact with her to this day. She helped me to learn so many valuable lessons that I have since lovingly implemented into how I live my life.

Somehow, despite my fear, I got into a routine in

prison. I was going to the gym and writing a lot, spending time re-evaluating what life meant to me, and what direction I wanted my life to take. I knew that the life that I had been leading was certainly not for me. You could say that I wanted to be born again. I knew something big had to change for a new life, a new direction and a new vibration to take hold of me. I wanted it and absolutely wasn't going to let anything to stand in my way of achieving it.

My brother flew all the way over to Ibiza to visit me from Sydney, Australia. At the point I really knew (if I ever needed to know) that he loved me and cared for me deeply. With him he brought a care package - a photo of my mum, some warm clothes and two books, *The Alchemist* and *The Pilgrimage,* both by Paulo Coelho.

Up until now I had never been a reader but knew that this was time to start.

The Alchemist changed the way I view life and helped re-form the foundations of who I am and where I want to be in life. *The Pilgrimage* opened my eyes and heart to my connection with God and to myself. It became the pivotal inspiration to go and experience the Camino De Santiago. In September 2017 I fulfilled that dream that I had cherished for 11 years.

people that we had arrived. Grappling with my case, I got off the bus and crossed the road to get a bus back and when that bus reached Alcudia I realised that it was still a long walk down to the port. I was a bit fed up by this time. Then I saw a man with a horse and cart and asked if he would take me. When he told me he was going to India I told him a bit about it before he dropped me off.

During the four-hour long wait for the ferry to Minorca I got talking to a lady from France. It was the first time she had been away on her own. She told me how she and her two sons had been in a very bad car accident. Now one of them was a paraplegic and she had metal in both legs and one ankle. People didn't help her, she said, because they couldn't see that there was anything wrong with her.

We had a rough crossing but luckily for me I was able to lie down when two people decided to move and free up some space. I wondered if this was the universe at work because I am okay on heavy seas as long as I can lie down. The French lady felt awful when she arrived. She had been sitting up.

When we came to disembark I was told where to go to get a taxi, but it was quite a long way to walk with my case. I believe the angels were at work to help me again, though. The other lady had booked a shuttle bus to the taxi rank and the shuttle bus driver, thinking that we were together, just put my case into the minibus.

I had booked to stay two nights at the Hotel Mar Blava, Ciutadella. It's a small family run hotel run by two brothers and a school friend from when they were 6 years old. They were so friendly and helpful and really made their guests feel at home. I was very happy with my room overlooking a sea inlet and a view of the sunset, so I asked if I could stay for the week. They said they were pretty full, but somehow I felt that there would be a room for me. I got the last one.

I had persuaded Natacha to come for a night while I was there. When I enquired about this they told me there was a back room available that she could have, near mine. I didn't book it for her, though, until the night before she came. Miraculously, it was still available. Amazing what happens when you go with the flow!

'The universe has done it again. The perfect place, near a vegetarian restaurant, that I found on the internet; near the town and buses. So grateful! Ciutadella is a beautiful town with narrow streets to meander around, with different coloured houses. There is a beautiful cathedral and monastery which you can visit together on one ticket.'

I had gone to Menorca to see if I could walk round the island, but found it was not going to be easy. The best time to walk is in winter, but of course many of the hotels are closed then. Also there is a 34-kilometre long stretch where there is absolutely nothing and not even the possibility of finding a taxi.

I decided to just enjoy walking some of the footpaths.

There were a lot of urbanisations to walk through before you could leave Ciutadella, and they weren't very pretty, so I got a taxi to Cala Blanca and started walking from there. It was a beautiful day. I walked for an hour and a half over hard ground and rock that looked like lava. It was hard walking but there were many plants, and I thought how lovely it must be in spring. I walked to the lighthouse at D'Artrutx and stopped there at the restaurant for a much needed rest and drink.

On the Monday I walked to Cala Galdana and through pinewoods to Cala Macarella. It was a beautiful walk with autumn crocus brightening the edges of the path. I was heading for a viewpoint where it was possible to see two beaches. The beautiful turquoise water backed by the lush green pine trees, a yacht floating in the bay made a magical scene that will remain forever in my memory.

I followed the path through the woods and down some steep steps, and reached the beach. After a swim in the pristine clear water and a picnic on the beach a thought came to me to go to the restaurant for a drink while I let my swimsuit dry off a bit.

I sat there for quite a while. When it was time to go I cleaned my feet of sand and put on my boots. As I was leaving I asked a man how to find the path from the restaurant then set off and walked a few feet before stopping to change out of my wet swimming costume. Just then the man that I had spoken to in the restaurant came and started to talk to me. His name was Nick.

When I had finished changing we walked together to the path that would take me back to Cala Galdana. "What a coincidence that we met," he said. I replied simply, "Nothing is coincidence." After we had been talking for a while he invited me to spend a day with him. He had a car and would take me to an isolated beach at Trebulgar, which was about an hour's walk away from the car park nearest to it.

I had been channelled that I would meet a man soon. Natacha had said that she had a vision of me meeting a man in Menorca.

Natacha was coming on the Tuesday and Wednesday,

so Nick and I arranged to meet on Thursday.

It had taken lot of persuasion to get Natacha to leave her farm for two days but she was so happy once she got there. We did two lovely walks.

On one of the days we took a bus to San Sarria where there is a beautiful, long, sandy, silver beach with pristine turquoise water. We had a swim and kept our costumes on while we walked to Turquesa beach nearby. Just then a tourist boat arrived with hoards of people, some going to this beach, some walking to the one we were heading for. Our silence was shattered. Still so busy, even in September!

Thursday came. I went to meet Nick at the cathedral and we drove to a car park just outside Cala Galdana for our expedition to Trebulgar Beach. As I was getting out of the car I looked behind me to see two cars, one with a 3777 number plate and the other with the number 3377. "Is this a sign?" I asked myself. Then I laughed when the first thing he took out of the car was an olive wood walking stick. After the channelling I'd had with her, Solara had said that she could see a man with a walking stick. He had the stick! Not because he was old, but because he liked walking with one. Was this another sign?

Nick likes to walk in nature in quiet and so do I.

We saw quite a few butterflies. One was quite rare, called Pasha, and there was also a yellow one with what looked like green on it. There were Swallowtails and a brown one that had spots. It looked like a Meadow Brown, but smaller. I decided to buy a book on the butterflies of Europe. I have always wanted to encourage butterflies, insects, dragonflies, and birds to be part of the scene on my land, when I have found it.

We stopped for a picnic in the woods before we reached the beach. It was a most beautiful beach with deep turquoise sea backed by pine trees. There was quite a climb down to the beach over rocks and through a long beautiful tunnel to reach a river that we waded across to get to the beach. After we'd had a swim in the pristine waters Nick showed me a place where I could sit in the shade.

'I have changed my thoughts about Menorca now as the south is really magnificent.'

After a while Nick said he wanted to paint and suggested that I walk through the woods on a sandy path. I could go barefoot, he said, and I would get a surprise.

As I walked out of the trees I was amazed to see a lake full of reeds, surrounded by steep stone cliffs and pine trees fronting the rocks. It was a magical spot - and teeming with wildlife.

I sat and meditated for I don't know how long because I didn't have my watch. In the quiet I heard a fish jump. The ducks flapped and chatted. Birds were flying around the lake.

When I returned I found that Nick had painted a picture of a tree with the sea as a background. He told me how, the first time he'd gone to that beach some years ago, the only other people there had been two young women. It must have been great to be so quiet. He had painted a picture of the beach with the two girls on it and shown them the painting. Then he'd asked them to sign it. Now he has the painting in his house.

Two days later I caught the 10 o'clock boat back to Mallorca. It was a big boat much better suited for rough seas than the small one that I had taken to get to Menorca. We passed the small boat going the other way. It would have been the 14:00 boat that I might have taken had there not been a charge for changing my booking. Now I had the answer - I had not been meant to go on the small boat.

The taxi from the port back to Natacha's house cost me €34 - the exact sum that I had been asked to pay to change my ferry ticket! There are no coincidences!

The following morning Natacha took me to the port to catch the boat back to Ibiza. When I showed my ticket to embark they told me that I had to change it, but couldn't explain why.

That meant going down and up the steps, so I left my case at the top rather than lug it down and up again. Then I had to wait to change my ticket. It was all making me feel quite stressed.

Eventually, when all was done and I was aboard, I asked someone why I'd had to do all that. The lady told me that the scheduled boat that I'd originally been booked on had been cut. This was a high-speed boat and would arrive in Ibiza in just two hours instead of the usual three-and-a-half or four hours. How lucky is that!

I sat looking out of the window of the boat, watching the sun coming up. There was a slight mist and foam sprayed up by the boat as it moved across a sea that was as smooth as ice. It was quite magical!

We didn't seem to be going very fast. Then I went outside, to the stern of the boat. Wow! There were huge sprays of water that could have only

been thrown out by a boat travelling at immense speed. As I watched, I meditated to tune in to the energy of the water.

chapter forty one

Satsang with Master Samdarshi

Everything happens with perfect timing.

Before I had gone to Mallorca, Karima had asked me if I would like to join a two-day long meditation retreat with Master Samdarshi. I did not know what to expect, but everything comes at the right time - and so it was on this occasion too.

On the first day we had Satsang. Not everyone at Satsang was also on the retreat. The Master explained that, to bring light into our lives, it is important to meditate for an hour everyday, at the same time. After Satsang we had an hour of yoga dance and then we relaxed afterwards.

Next the Master told us we should do whatever we wanted to bring up our anger. It would be a "crazy madhouse." We could talk gobbledegook, shout, scream, bash a pillow - anything that would release suppressed feelings.

In the afternoon, after a vegan lunch in the garden, we did Kundalini meditation - shaking the whole body for half hour and then easy dance to music. This is something that I had done at Osho's in India and it's something that I love doing.

On the second day we did meditation dance and then we laughed for twenty minutes. I was next to a lovely man from Kazakhstan called Sultan Madan. He made me laugh so much that my stomach hurt. I am certain that it was no coincidence that he was next to me. Then we had to cry for twenty minutes. As I was stopping crying I felt a ripple of energy in my forehead and I knew it was my spiritual guide Ehab. That's when I really started crying because I remembered him telling me, when I first met him, that I needed to purify myself by crying. After the crying time we remained in silence for twenty minutes.

Later I wrote, *'Moved a lot of stuff. I feel so good now.'*

Master told us that this was just a preliminary exercise. In India people laugh for one week, cry for one week and are then silent for one week. I think this would be difficult.

After that morning session we took the boat from Es Canar to Santa Eulalia and walked along the seafront to have lunch at a seafront restaurant. In the afternoon we did more shaking. We ended the day with another Satsang in the evening as the sun was going down and the full moon was coming up. Magic!

As I was walking into the ashram on the second day I saw a car with 9999 on the number plate. I checked the angel meaning of the number in my angel book. It read, "This is the completion of a chapter in your life and now it is time to get to work, without procrastination, on your next life chapter." I realised that a cycle of my life was coming to an end.

chapter forty two

Solara Marries Gino

Solara channelled the information from her Star guides that she would meet her man as soon as she had concluded her autobiography, *Pleiadian Emissary to Gaia*. She was having difficulty with the writing at the time, so the guidance was exactly the carrot on a stick that she needed to finish her story. Her guides encouraged her by explaining that until she finished telling the story of her journey thus far she would not be able to enter the new chapter of her life with the partner that for so many years she had been longing for.

When she finally succeeded in finishing her book in October 2016, she was keen to celebrate by travelling to Bali. But the guidance was very clear – wait until December to start the trip, and go to Thailand first. She would come to understand why that had been the guidance later.

Once in Thailand she went to Pai in the north of the country and met..... Gino. This wonderful man was, indeed, everything that she had been waiting for! There was just one small problem – he was French and spoke hardly any English. At first this was quite a challenge but when Solara dusted off her schoolgirl French and started, falteringly at first, to use it to talk to him, she was surprised, amazed and delighted at how easily it came back. She had the feeling that she was really being assisted. Within a few weeks of their first meeting she was speaking fluently!

The day after their first meeting, Gino was due to travel further north, and had already booked his bus ticket. Solara had planned to go to a retreat for the following three days. She asked Gino to take her on the back of his motorbike to the retreat venue before he left, which he did. Then they went their separate ways but once he had left Gino could not stop the voice in his head that was plaguing him, repeating over and over, 'Go back to Pai! Go back to Pai!' So, even though he wasn't sure if she was at all attracted to him, he felt compelled to listen to that inner command. He knew where to find Solara at the retreat venue – and ended up joining the workshop that Solara was participating in, despite the fact that it was in English.

The universe worked its magic on both of them. In a *Family Constellation* session all of Solara's resistances to accepting a new love were dissolved.

Just one year after she had completed her book, on 14th October 2017, Solara and Gino were married.

The ceremony took place on the beautiful yoga platform in her Ibiza garden. Gino called it a "rebel wedding." There were neither priest nor formalities, just the heart-felt declarations of love and commitment that came naturally from their hearts in the moment. Solara looked beautiful in her white dress with a floral garland on her head and flowers from her garden in her hands.

The small group of friends and family who attended sat in a circle, as we always do on sacred occasions on the island, so that all can share equally and contribute to the energy of the group. Afterwards we passed a flower around the circle as a form of talking stick and each in turn gave congratulations to the newly-weds. Several of us cried at the sheer beauty of it all.

Once the ceremonials were over we shared a wonderful pot luck lunch. Later Solara and her daughter sang while Gino, who is a musician, played electric guitar.

I felt so blessed to be part of the ceremony and this wonderful group of people. It will be great when we live near each other and can play music together and have fun – for isn't that what life is all about.

chapter forty-three

A Chapter Closes, A New One Opens

What happens next is pretty mind-boggling.

I wanted some clarity about Nick and I needed to know if I was meant to go to Portugal to live, where Solara was now planning to go, so I went for a channelling.

I was told that reaching Compostela marked the end of a life chapter. I would be going to Portugal to live in a community and teach permaculture. Nick is an old soul that I have been together with in a past life, but I am moving into higher consciousness at a fast rate, while he is slower. I was also told that I needed to build myself up to be strong because I had a lot of work to do. I was told that my children would come and see what I was doing and think I was "normal" again.

For many years it has been my dream to build an earth

ship. I had wanted to do it on Ibiza, but was blocked at every turn. I wanted to buy land but there turned out to be no hope of that on the island. Property prices had turned out to be astronomical. Legislation about new builds and accommodation was tight and restrictive

For five long years I tried to find land to build an earth ship there, and to create a permaculture fruit forest. Now I started looking forward to going to Portugal where I would be able to buy land and where there would be government help for people wanting to set up a community.

I wanted to fulfil my dream of building an earth ship, working together with other people to build each other's homes from recycled materials such as tyres, bottles, and cans. What a difference it would make to mother earth if we were to use more of what we have without decimating the planet by exploiting her limited resources.

I love Ibiza so much and I feel very blessed to have lived here for five years, in a place where you can come up spiritually in one year where you would need five elsewhere. It taught me a great deal but left me deeply saddened by the way it is being ruined.

Even as we build and make progress, we need to do so